Charters and Caldicott

As War Begins

Peter Storey

This book is dedicated to Julie

Contents

Acknowledgements

Great thanks must go to Frank Launder and Sidney Gilliat, the film writers who first created Charters and Caldicott and also to Basil Radford and Naunton Wayne who brought them to life in film after film – they made the characters their own!

Researching and writing this tribute to the characters of Charters and Caldicott has been a long and enjoyable experience; partly because of the many times that I have watched the films featuring the two chaps and also because of all the new and exciting bits of information that my research led to. However, the most enjoyable part has been talking to family and friends about the book and having illuminating conversations with them about the films and what they enjoy about them. I would like to thank all these people for the help, encouragement and support in my research and writing.

In particular, I would like to thank my son Ben and daughter Sarah for sharing my enthusiasm for films and their company when watching them. But without my wife Julie, who also happens to be my best friend, this book would never have happened. Not only does she share my enthusiasm for films, she has motivated and encouraged me with words of wisdom, loving support and endless cups of coffee, even though at times she probably felt that Charters and Caldicott had taken up residence in our home. For all this and much more, I dedicate this book to Julie.

If you enjoy watching the films featuring Charters and Caldicott, then I hope that you enjoy reading this book. If you want to know more about the two chaps, you might want to visit the Charters and Caldicott website www.chartersandcaldicott.co.uk

The author also welcomes feedback by email at administrator@chartersandcaldicott.co.uk

Author's note

Growing up in England during the 1960's and 1970's, I was engrossed by the black and white films that dominated television on weekend afternoons. The films that I watched invariably revolved around the Second World War, whether in the events leading up to it, during it or in the years following as Britain and Europe attempted to recover from the devastation that war inevitably wrought. My viewing comprised many films covering the whole sphere of life during this period, both of the adventures of the British at war in Europe or of life on the home front.

There were lots of variations of themes, films about battles at sea, on land or in the air, films about resistance fighters and films of spies and espionage. Whether set in one of the many other European countries caught up in the conflict, the locations seemed as far apart in distance from where I grew up as they were in time for my generation. Films that stand out include The Dam Busters, The Lady Vanishes, Ice Cold in Alex and Night Train To Munich plus many others. There were other films of the same era, but set in locations much closer to home focusing on life on the Home Front, such as Went The Day Well, A Canterbury Tale and Millions Like Us.

For generations of viewers, these films are timeless classics, continuing to be shown not only on television, but also in their original home of cinemas up and down the country. Why do people continually enjoy watching these films? For many, including myself, it is not the subject of war itself, but the characters that feature in them. The film's characters generally had the same traits; firstly they showed the resilience of the British people in the face of adversity with their stiff upper lip approach to the turmoil's they faced. Secondly, the characters possessed charming accents that one never hears outside of the films, using phrases such as old chap or old boy when addressing each other or calling someone a cad as an insult.

But it isn't just the language or the film setting that draws me to them, it is the desire to know more about the characters and the stories that they have yet to tell, long after the credits finish rolling at the end of the film. Of the films listed above, three of them feature the two same characters, namely Charters and Caldicott, like many people the world over, I want to know more about them, what they did, where they went and also what became of them.

The characters are amongst film history's most famous and favourite comedy duos – up there with the likes of Laurel and Hardy or Morecambe and Wise – but without the slapstick. Full of English idiosyncrasies, they represent a bygone era of the 1940's. These two gentlemen have a love of cricket and are sticklers for upholding proper standards of dress, decorum and behaviour. Charters and Caldicott's comedy approach in responding to the military might of the enemy's aggressions were a forerunner of other comedies, most notably Dads Army.

Charters and Caldicott may not have been part of the direct British war effort, but they played an essential part in undermining and defeating the enemy. As on screen characters, they poked fun at the Third Reich and made light of the ridiculousness of their military and authoritarian rule as they marched across Europe. By undermining the enemy on screen, the duo helped to keep morale high at home at a time when Britain was suffering heavy defeats.

The films they appeared in, notably The Lady Vanishes and Night Train to Munich are often listed in the top favourite films of all times. The directors, produces and writes of the movies, Alfred Hitchcock, Carol Reed, Sidney Gilliat and Frank Launder are equally listed as the most influential artists not just of their time but of their genre. The films regularly appear in top 100 lists compiled by film fans and critics the world over even through to the present day more than 70 years after they were first screened. Any simple search of the web will confirm this, not just in the UK, but the world over. The movies are regularly rescreened at cinemas throughout the world, bringing the characters to a growing audience.

What ties the love and admiration of these movies and artists together, are the two characters of Charters and Caldicott.

Introduction

This is neither a book about actors, nor the films that they appear in. Equally it is not a biography about film stars. So what is the book about? The only way to describe it, is to say that it is a biography of two fictional characters or rather the book is a detailed account of two fictional characters as they appeared in a series of films between the late 1930's and the 1940's. Who are these two fictional characters that can justify a biography? – They are of course Charters and Caldicott.

Charters and Caldicott, played brilliantly by Basil Radford and Naunton Wayne, first appeared in Hitchcock's The Lady Vanishes. The Lady Vanishes film is based on Ethel White's novel, The Wheel Spins. The original story did not feature the Charters and Caldicott characters; they were created specifically for the film by the writers Frank Launder and Sidney Gilliat.

From this first appearance in 1938, Charters and Caldicott soon became one of film history's most famous and favourite comedy duo, appearing in Night Train to Munich (1940) and Crook's Tour (1941). Full of English idiosyncrasies, Charters and Caldicott represent a bygone era of the 1930's and 1940's. Whilst they frequently travel around Europe, they are generally clueless about foreigners, their languages or their customs. These two English gentlemen are happy being English, or rather British; they have a love of cricket and are sticklers for upholding proper standards of dress, decorum and behaviour at all times. They are loved the world over for their excellent representation of being British in the seemingly black, white and grey era shown throughout the films of the era. Their manners are impeccable, except when they are being quietly or subversively rude, particularly when dealing with foreigners. They are well travelled, but their impolite indifference of foreigners, whether European, American or of anyone who is not British, is a delight to behold. They are well educated, but their ignorance of national languages or customs that are not of English or British origin is the complete opposite. One of the most endearing attributes of these two characters is their sense of fair play, most likely gained through their public school and Oxbridge education but more likely reinforced through their enthusiasm and love of the English game of cricket.

The duo, whilst well-groomed and educated at Oxford, are snobbish and self-regarding. At first glance they appear as a pair of bumbling upper class fools travelling around Europe ambivalent to the events developing around them; all this set in the period leading up to the Second World War and during the time known as the 'Phoney War'. It appears as though they were dreamt up by the German high command as a derogatory cameo of British foolishness as a means of war propaganda to undermine the British nerve. What they actually reflect is the British stiff upper lip in the face of adversity; they move almost seamlessly from their own cricket obsessed world to become enduring defenders of their view of the British way of life by directly engaging the enemies in whichever adventure they get caught up in. Their dry sense of humour, bordering on sarcasm, by gently making light of foreigners, is an absolute delight to watch.

Wherever they are in the world, Charters and Caldicott only want to be left alone in their own private British way. Mostly, they manage to travel as they desire, quietly watching and observing the world around them, enjoying their own company and conversations of cricket matches played and yet to be played. Whatever journey they are on, events around them come to the fore. Each time unplanned events unfold, they are initially reluctant to become involved, not because of cowardice or wanting to sit on the fence – these terms are anathema to Charters and Caldicott, but by becoming participants, they fear that they may be delayed from watching their next cricket match. When an 'adventure' comes their way, their sense of fair play overcome any initial doubts and they rise to defend the defenceless, quietly becoming the heroes of the hour. Idiosyncratic as they are, Charters and Caldicott, rise to the challenge before retiring quietly back to their gentlemanly world of cricket and conversations of past glories on the crease. In truth, and behind their understated humour, they represent how Britain alone, stood up to the might of the German Third Reich jack booting across Europe.

This is the first time ever that the exploits of Charters and Caldicott have been brought together in one book. This book is not about the stories of the movies, but is about the scenes that Charters and Caldicott appear in and live in. Line by line and word by word, this book is about what Charters and Caldicott see, hear and know about.

It is in effect the world that matters to them. In their world, innocent as they are, Charters and know nothing of the so-called 'bigger picture' and that is what makes them so agreeable and lovable.

Following their first appearance in Alfred Hitchcock's The Lady Vanishes in 1938, they proved popular with audiences and returned in the Gilliat and Launder films Night Train to Munich (1940) and Millions Like Us (1943), and in the BBC radio serials Crook's Tour (1941, made into a film later that year) and Secret Mission 609 (1942).

They were also intended to reappear as Charters and Caldicott in I See a Dark Stranger (1945), but the actors and producers could not agree on the larger roles that Radford and Wayne demanded. This resulted in the actors opting out of the film and consequently two similar but differently named characters were substituted. However, the disagreement left Basil Radford and Naunton Wayne contractually prevented from portraying the characters of Charters and Caldicott in further movies. Not to be thwarted, and in true Charters and Caldicott style, Radford and Wayne continued to play near identical characters in several other movies but with different names. They played similar double acts in several more movies, such as Dead of Night (1946), A Girl in a Million (1946) and Quartet (1948). Another recurring cricket mad pairing played by them were Bright and Early in It's Not Cricket (1949), Helter Skelter (1949) followed by Passport to Pimlico 1949) and Stop Press Girl (1949)

'As War Begins' covers the first four films that Charters and Caldicott appeared in between 1938 and 1941 –The Lady Vanishes, Night Train to Munich, Crook's Tour and Millions Like Us.

The Lady Vanishes

The Maid's room

Charters and Caldicott are sitting in the hotel reception area and not entirely happy about their predicament. They should be on their way back to England for an important appointment; an appointment that they are dearly looking forward to and one that has been in their diary for a long time. This unexpected and unwelcome break in their journey is a result of the weather. Like all Englishmen they enjoy talking about the weather and like all Englishmen talking about the weather, they are not happy about it. If it is raining, they will talk about how much rain has fallen and bemoaning the lack of sunshine; if it is sunny, they will complain about it being too hot and wondering when rain will next fall to help water the lawn

They are here in the hotel reception, after having to get off the train due to the railway line being blocked by snow from a spring avalanche. Sitting there watching the comings and goings, wondering when the train will resume its' journey, they watch as a little old lady opens the door and leaves the warmth of the hotel for the cold spring wind blowing outside. Opening the door, the two Englishmen are coolly reminded of the weather outside, as gusts of spring wind blows through the doorway and across the foyer. And then she's gone, closing the door behind her blocking out the wind.

Slowly, the chill disappears as the warmth from the open fire spreads back across the foyer. With nothing to do but wait for some sort of announcement about when their journey will resume, they continue sitting there as time slowly moves on; Charters smokes his pipe whilst his friend smokes a cigarette. The hotel clock chimes, or rather a trumpeter figure comes out of the clock in the same manner as a cuckoo would out of a cuckoo clock. Instead of a cuckoo from a bird, the clock sounds a hoot from the trumpet. As the trumpeter blows, Charters and Caldicott observe a waiter and porter chattering away in their foreign language; foreign to the two English men but local to Bandrika, the country where they now find themselves.

It is the same throughout the whole hotel foyer area, not one word of English is spoken, not even from Charters and Caldicott who sit there quietly observing the various comings and goings. In the silence, they hear a telephone ringing and the two Englishmen look over to the reception desk to see it being answered by a man they presume to be the hotel manager. The man answers the call in the local language of Bandrikan; after replacing the handset he speaks out loudly to the waiting groups. Just as Charters and Caldicott are waiting there for the train to continue its journey; many others of various nationalities are too, and just like the two Englishmen, not all of them understand Bandrikan. Fortunately, the manager shouts out his message in another language, Charters thinks possibly Italian. Most people hear and understand the message conveyed in the two languages as they start rushing towards the reception desk; but not the two Englishmen.
"What's all the fuss about Charters?" asks Caldicott.
"Damned if I know". Replies Charters

The Hotel Manager completes the announcement in a third language, which to Charters and Caldicott sounds like German. The Hotel Manager then proceeds to speak in English, "If you wish to stay in my hotel then you will have to register immediately".
Caldicott snaps "Why the deuce didn't he say so in the first place?"

Both he and Charters walk towards the reception desk and both smile in order to greet the equally smiling manager as he walks towards them. Their smile soon turns to a bemused look as the Hotel Manager walks straight past them and totally ignores them. Unsure about what has just happened, the two Englishmen turn to see what he is up to; they see him greet three young ladies who have just entered the hotel. They seem to know the Manager as they warmly greet him using his name Boris in their greeting. Charters and Caldicott continue to watch the proceedings, as Boris the Hotel Manager explains in English to the three young ladies that the railway is blocked due to an avalanche.

Continuing to ignore the presence of the two Englishmen, Boris, the Hotel Manager, accompanies the three young ladies up the stairs as they climb the stairs, chattering away and telling him what food and drink they want in their room. Charters and Caldicott continue to watch and overhear parts of the list which includes chicken, a magna of champagne, potatoes, bread followed by a humorous instruction to make it snappy.

Charters turns to Caldicott and drily says "Meanwhile, we have to stand here clicking our heels, eh! Confounded impudence"

They continue to stand there looking at the girls walking up the stairs giving their food orders to Boris, before turning to look at the hotel reception which whilst unstaffed, is overcrowded by all the other guests. After momentarily pondering about what his friend has just said and the sight before him at the reception desk, Caldicott says "Its a third rate country, what do you expect?"
"I wonder who those women were?" says Charters.
"Possibly Americans, I should think" replies Caldicott, "You know? Almighty dollar!" his friend nods in agreement.
"I suppose we will just have to wait here. If only we hadn't missed that train at Budapest", says Charters.
"I don't want to rub it in, but if you hadn't insisted on standing up until they had finished their national anthem" says Caldicott drily.
Charters tries to explain his behaviour in Budapest "Yes, but you must show respect Caldicott. Besides If I'd known it was going to last twenty minutes"
Caldicott interrupts him and says "It has always been my contention that the Hungarian Rhapsody is not their national anthem. In any case, we were the only two standing".
Charters nods in agreement, adding "That's true".

Slightly annoyed by the mistake innocently made by his friend made but slightly more embarrassed about openly criticising him, Caldicott changes the subject and says "Well, I suppose we shall be in time won't we" referring to their appointment back in England that they are desperate to get back for.
"I doubt it" says Charters "that last report was pretty ghastly. Do you remember? England on the brink!"
"Yes but that is newspaper sensationalism" replies Caldicott. "The old country has been in some tight corners before".
"It still looks pretty black, even if we get away first thing tomorrow morning. There's still the connection at Basle. We'll probably be hours" adds Charters. "That's true" agrees Caldicott.

Looking up, Charters says "Well, surely somebody can help us" as he walks over to a man who looks as though he works at the hotel. Caldicott turns to follow him as Charters asks the man, "Oh sir, can you tell us what time the train leaves Basle for England?"

The man replies "nein sprachense England"

"Oh really" Charters says. "The fellow doesn't speak English"

Neither of the two speaks any other language, as being British they do not really see the need for it. Being British, they both expect other nationalities, or rather foreigners, to be able to speak English. Disappointed at the man's lack of ability to speak English and not knowing what to say next, they both look away, downhearted that they are still no nearer to finding out what is happening to England.

Boris, the Hotel Manager, returns to reception where the rush of people to the desk starts again as the other stranded passengers try to book rooms. Meanwhile, Caldicott is standing at the edge of the reception desk where he overhears the manager order food and champagne for the young ladies that he had just escorted upstairs. He is hungry and overhearing the conversation about food, he dreams of putting in his own order for food and sitting down to enjoy a splendid meal. While he is half dreaming of food whilst simultaneously listening to the manager's conversation, Charters is at the back of the crowd unsuccessfully trying to gently push his way to the front.

He continues to leave his friend to sort out the hotel reservation; he diverts his attention to reading a train timetable which he sees laying towards the end of the reception desk. Charters, sees what he is reading and edges over to where Caldicott is standing; he says "We leave Basle at 21:20". Rather than booking a room, they find the timetable more interesting and they both concentrate on reading the timetable. Charters retrieves his fob watch from his pocket and counts around the dial trying to convert time from the 24 hour clock listings in order to make more sense of the train times.

The queue at the reception desk is much reduced and Caldicott fins that it his turn to speak to the Hotel Manager, "We need a private suite with a bath" he says.

"Facing the mountains" adds Charters.

Caldicott continues "With a shower of course"

18

"Hot and cold" adds Charters.

The Manager listens to what the two Englishmen have been requesting and forlornly flicks through his reservations book, whilst Caldicott continues with their room requirements by adding "And a private thingummy, if you've got one?"

Charters and Caldicott try to reserve a room with Boris the Hotel Manager (Emile Boreo)

Boris doesn't need to look through his book as he already knows the answer; having gone through the motions for appearance sake, he looks up and says "I'm sorry gentlemen; the only thing I've got is the maid's room".

Charters exclaims "You what!" and looks at Caldicott.

The Manager explains "I am sorry; the whole hotel is jammed, jammed to the top" and waves his right arm in the air as if to explain better.

Caldicott is not happy "But that is impossible, we haven't fixed up yet"

"Anyway, you can't expect to put us up in the maid's room" adds Charters. The Manager responds by saying "Oh, don't get excited, I will remove the maid out!"

Not happy with the Manager's impudence, Charters retorts "Oh, I should think so. What?, what are you talking about?"

Caldicott adds "Look here, I think I should rather sleep on the train. Wouldn't you?", he looks at Charters for agreement.

The Manager says "There is no eating on the train"

"No eating on the train?" asks a bemused Caldicott.

After a slight delay, whilst he thinks of another way of describing what he wants to say, and fails to do so, the Manager repeats "Yes no eating on the train. Brrr, brrr" adding the last bit as a better means of explanation.

Caldicott now understands and says "Oh, no heating. He means no heating on the train".

Charters says "Oh, Oh that's awkward. Alright we'll take it".

"Just a minute, there is one condition" says the Manager, "you will have to have the maid come to your room and remove her wardrobe" as he indicates to his own clothes with his hands. He then shouts and gesticulates for the maid to come over to where they are standing, "Anna".

Charters and Caldicott look at each other, clearly confused and uncertain of what has just been said, particularly about Anna and her wardrobe, at what it all means and more worryingly, what they have just agreed to.

Anna soon arrives and the Hotel Manager says to the Englishmen "She's a good girl and I don't want to lose her".

He continues by saying something in Bandrikan to Anna, before cheekily pinching her cheek and indicating Charters and Caldicott to her. They look back at her, still confused and very uncertain as to what has just been agreed. Anna gives them a big cheeky smile, raises her eyebrows and nods her head. Charters and Caldicott are both perturbed by this over familiarity, their mouths drop and they look at each other with a worried expression; both thinking how are they going to tackle this very delicate and potentially embarrassing situation.

Charters says quietly to Caldicott "We'd better go and get dressed" Caldicott collects his coat off the reception desk and they both walk across the foyer. Out of earshot from the hotel manager at the reception desk, Caldicott says "Rather primitive humour I thought" "Or grown up children" adds Charters, "A rather tricky situation over that girl" Caldicott says "A pity he couldn't have given us one each"

"Eh?" asks Charters, perturbed by his friend's seemingly risqué request. "I mean a room each" says Caldicott.

"Oh" says his relieved friend as they both walk towards the stairs.

A short while later the two friends are in their hotel room unpacking their cases which are laid side by side on the bed. They discuss the worrying events back in England, with Charters saying "Its' the hanging around that is getting to me. If only we knew what was happening in England"

"Mustn't lose grip Charters", says Caldicott as he tries to placate him. Caldicott checks his shirt collar but there is a knock on the hotel room door which diverts his attention. "Come in" says Charters, quickly goes to get his jacket which is hanging on the back of the door – he considers it only proper that he should be appropriately dressed when greeting visitors in his room, even if he is sharing with Caldicott..

It is Anna the maid who enters and says what appears to the two Englishmen as hello, but in Bandrikan. Charters and Caldicott turn to look at each other, both concerned at the arrival of the young woman and equally uncomfortable with the idea of an un-chaperoned young woman being in their bedroom, maid or no maid.

She doesn't say anything else to the two men, but merely concentrates on collecting her belongings from the room. This task involves her bending over in front of the two men. Charters and Caldicott presume that she is retrieving a chamber pot or something of a similar personal nature and they look at each other wondering what to do. Being gentlemen, they both avert their eyes by quickly turning round to face the other way. As they hurriedly turn, Caldicott accidently drops his pyjamas – they land not on the floor but into a basin of washing water. Charters tries to indicate to Caldicott what has happened, but unfortunately he is too embarrassed to discuss his nightwear in front of the maid and instead fiddles with his bow tie. Fortunately for Charters and Caldicott, when they turn around, they see that it is not a chamber pot that she has retrieved but a hat from a hat box that was stored under the bed.

Wearing the hat and smiling, Anna says something, again in Bandrikan, but as they know no language other than English, Charters and Caldicott fail to understand her. Caldicott asks of Charters "Did you follow all that?"

His friend obviously did or rather thinks he did, "I did" he says, "Tell her this has gone far enough".

Anna the maid (Kathleen Tremaine) comes to remove her 'wardrobe' from Charters and Caldicott's hotel room.

Caldicott ties to, but uses his hands in the way that an Englishman typically does to emphasise what he wants to say when talking to foreigners. "There is no change here, err no change, no change here!" he says. To avoid any further confusion on the maid's part, he adds "erm outside, outside".

Anna is oblivious to what is being said and starts to remove her top. Charters, whilst shocked, looks disdainfully at Caldicott who in his view has not tried explaining the situation well enough. "She doesn't understand" Caldicott says by way of an explanation.

Charters steps in to try and explain himself, "No, come on" indicating with his head towards the door; this is a hint for the two gentlemen to leave the room. Unfortunately for Charters, when he goes to open the door, he bangs his head on the low beam and responds with an "oh!"

An apprehensive Caldicott follows Charters out of the hotel room but before doing so he turns to look at the maid, uncertain as to what to say.

Cricket Sir. Cricket!

No true English gentleman would contemplate not being properly attired for dinner. Outside on the landing, Charters and Caldicott are almost, but not quite, suitably dressed. The two men, having collected their dinner jackets on their way out of the room, need to finish dressing. Caldicott puts his jacket on while Charters' still hangs on a wooden hanger in his hand. After taking his jacket from the hanger, Charters hands it to Caldicott who at this point only has the one arm in a jacket sleeve. Caldicott takes the hanger from Charters but carries on putting his jacket on whilst Charters starts to put his on too. Whilst Caldicott finishes putting his jacket on, he looks at the hanger that Charters gave him and wonders what on earth he has been given it for and also what to do with it. The obvious think for Caldicott is to return it to Charters who obligingly takes it off him. Caldicott now with both hands free is able to straighten his jacket and collar. However, the situation has been reversed and Charters now wonders what to do with the hanger; he looks disdainfully at Caldicott wondering why he has given the hanger back to him even though he can clearly see that he hasn't got his jacket on yet. The obvious solution is to put it on a low shelf which is conveniently to his side. Standing up from having stooped to put the hanger down, he bangs his head yet again on another low beam. Rubbing his head for the second time this evening, he looks at Caldicott, annoyed at his friend's discourteous lack of assistance. Finally and properly attired, the two descend the stairs.

In the hotel reception, they detect that other guests are looking at them with a rather peculiar manner. Charters and Caldicott cannot understand why this is the case, but they notice, disappointingly, that nobody else has bothered to dress for dinner. Unperturbed by the strange looks that they are receiving, they make their way over to the reception desk where Charters picks up a newspaper. He soon tosses it back down, "nothing newer than last month" he says.

23

Ignoring the question, Caldicott asks "I don't suppose there's such a thing as a wireless set here old boy?"

"I don't like being in the dark Caldicott. Our communications cut off in a time of crisis" his friend replies.

Charters looks for a newspaper or magazine that is written in English.

Looking around for a more recent English newspaper, or even a wireless set, they see the Boris the Hotel Manager at the reception desk talking on the telephone. Not deliberately listening, they overhear him loudly saying "Hallo, Hallo London". At the mention of London, Charters and Caldicott both simultaneously concentrate their hearing on what is being said. The Manager continues "You want Mr Seltzer? Yes, hold on, I'm going to find where he is".

Whilst the Manager leaves to find Mr Seltzer, Charters turns to Caldicott "London!" he exclaims

Momentarily pausing to look at each other, they both dash over to the phone. Before picking the receiver up, they again hesitatingly before looking around to see whether or not they are likely to be caught. Caldicott encouragingly says "Go on, risk it".

Charters acts on his friend's encouragement and picks up the receiver to start speaking "Hello, hello, you in London"
In response to the question from the other end of the line, Charters replies "What? No, no, I'm not Mr Seltzer. The name is Charters. I don't suppose you know me".

Charters is interrupted by the caller asking where the manager is, but continues "What? Well you needn't worry; he's just gone to fetch him. Tell me, what's happening to England?"

The caller refers to the weather and Charters retorts "Blowing a gale? You don't follow me sir, I'm enquiring about the test match in Manchester".
The caller clearly doesn't understand what Charters is referring to which enrages Charters; he shouts "Cricket Sir, Cricket!"

It is obvious that the caller doesn't know what is happening with cricket; Charters continues "You don't know, then you can't be in England and not know the Test score".
He places his hand over the receiver so he can talk to Caldicott "He doesn't know".
Caldicott, picking up oh his friend's comment is also not amused, "Oh silly man" he replies.

Charters tries again to get some sense from the caller by saying "Look, can't you find out. It won't take a second". Clearly exasperated by now he gives up on the conversation and finally says "Oh alright; if you won't, you won't" and slams the receiver back onto it's' cradle.
Turning to Caldicott, he says "Wasting my time, the fellow is an ignoramus".

They storm off, annoyed at the lack of interest in cricket shown by the caller and also at their continued ignorance in not knowing the test score. Fortunately, their behaviour was not seen by Boris the Hotel Manager who returns with another hotel guest, presumably the Mr Seltzer. The two Englishmen turn and look as the Manager picks up the phone and say to the hotel guest, "Mr Seltzer, at last your call's come through to London".

No.no, I'm not Mr Seltzer says Charters to the caller from Manchester

He shouts down the receiver, but to no avail, "Hello, Hello". Charters feels the need to say something to Caldicott about having replaced the receiver but thinks better of it. They both decide to turn a blind eye and feign innocence to their role in what has just happened and turn on their heels to walk through reception and across to the dining room.

The smoke filled dining room is very busy and Charters and Caldicott survey the room to look for an empty table, but there are none, not immediately anyway. After a short while, Charters sees an opportunity and indicates to Caldicott, a table, where some of the current occupiers are putting their coats on in readiness to leave. However, another group has also spotted the impending vacancy; if the two Englishmen are to get to the table first they must act fast. The two opposing groups jostle to get the recently vacated seats all the while the waiter concentrates on clearing the table. The two Englishmen win the race, Caldicott first, followed swiftly by Charters. The losing group of diners are clearly not impressed with this unexpected behaviour of the two Englishmen and look disdainfully at the now seated victors. The waiter, seeing what has happened, says something to Charters. Clearly not understanding a word of what was said to him, but thinking that the waiter had moved the other group along he says "Thank you waiter"

Again the waiter says something in Bandrikan. Presuming that the waiter is asking him what he wants to order, Charters turns to Caldicott and asks "What do you think to a grilled steak?"

Caldicott replies "A very good idea" and turns to the waiter "Well done please!"

Charters also decides on a steak and adds "On the rare side for me". Again the waiter tries to say something. It is clear that the waiter doesn't understand a word of English, nor do the two Englishmen understand a word of Bandrikan.

Charters leans over to his friend and says "These people have a passion for repeating themselves".

At this point, an old lady sat opposite Charters and Caldicott politely coughs and says "I beg your pardon" to which Charters mumbles a polite acknowledgement in return.

The old lady continues "He's trying to explain to you that owing to the large number of visitors, there is no food left".

"No food! What sort of place is this?" Charters snaps to no one in particular before turning to Caldicott in a quieter tone "they expect us to share a blasted dog box with a servant girl, on an empty stomach. Is that hospitality? Is that organisation?"

Charters forgets his manners in ignoring the elderly lady and collects himself. Turning to her, he says "Oh, thank you". At this point the waiter leaves in the knowledge that his explanations have now been translated and understood.

Caldicott starts to say to Charters "I'm hungry enough ... "

Before he can say what he would eat, he is interrupted by his friend retorting "What sort of a country, no wonder they are having a revolution"

The old lady continues to watch the two English travellers and after listening to their conversation offers her plate of food by saying "You are very welcome to have what is left of the cheese. Its' not like beef steak but it is awfully rich in vitamins".

27

Charters thanks the old lady "oh really, thank you very much".
The conversation continues with the old lady saying "I'm afraid that they are not accustomed to catering for so many people. Bandrika is one of Europe's undiscovered corners".
Charters is not convinced and says "That is because there is nothing worth discovering I think".

In defence of the country, the old lady replies "You may not know it as much as I do. I am feeling quite miserable at the thought of leaving it". Throughout this conversation Charters eats the cheese under the watchful eye of Caldicott who cuts in to the conversation by saying, "After you with the cheese please".
Charters, still eating the cheese, replies "Certainly old man, why not" but instead of passing the plate of cheese to his friend, he continues in his conversation with the old lady,
"You are going home?" he asks her.
"Tomorrow" she replies, "My little charges are quite grown up. I am a governess and a music teacher you know. In the six years that I have lived here I have grown to love the country. Especially the mountains, I sometimes think that they are like very friendly neighbours. You know, the big mother and father mountains, with their little white snow hats and their nephews and nieces, not so big with their smaller hats. Right down to the tiniest hillocks without any hats at all. Well of course that is just my fancy"

Tired and hungry, Charters and Caldicott find the conversation dull and slightly boring, to the extent that they rudely sit with their chins in their hands wondering what on earth the old lady is talking about. Realising his rudeness, Charters interrupts the old lady's monologue in order to add to the conversation, However, the only words that he can utter are "Oh really!"
The old lady continues "I like to watch them from my bedroom every night when there is a moon. I am so glad there is a moon tonight. Do you hear that music? Everyone sings here. The people are just like happy children with laughter on their lips and music in their heart". Charters interrupts again by saying "It's not reflected in their politics you know?"

"I never think you should judge a country by its politics you know" says the old lady, "after all, we English are quite honest by nature aren't we? If you will excuse me while I run away. Goodnight". The old lady picks up her bag, leaves and nods her head in acknowledgement, to another guest who has been sitting silently to the side of her. Remembering their manners, Charters and Caldicott stand as the old lady leaves; both say goodnight to her and smile politely at each other.

After the old lady has gone, Charters turns to Caldicott and says "A queer sort of bird".
"A trifle whimsical I thought" replies his friend.
"After six years in this hole, we would be whimsical" adds Charters. Caldicott disagrees "Oh, I don't think so old man. She was very decent about the cheese".
"I think we should finish the pickles" says Charters. Caldicott still has not had any cheese and annoyed with his friend he looks hungrily at the empty plate on the table in front of Charters. Charters has selfishly and greedily eaten it all without sharing.

Tired and hungry, Charters and Caldicott find the conversation dull and slightly boring

Gute Nacht

Back in their hotel room, the two Englishmen are in bed together reading the Herald and Tribune newspaper. "Nothing but baseball" says Caldicott "You know, they used to call it rounders. Children play it with a rubber ball and a stick. Not a word about cricket. The Americans don't know any sense of proportion" he continues.
A knock on the door interrupts Caldicott's views on Americans, baseball and their lack of sense of proportion. As he says "Come in", the two men put the newspaper down which they have been jointly reading, in order to see who will enter their room. Charters is wearing pyjamas, or rather a pyjama top, whilst Caldicott is wearing the corresponding pair of pyjama bottoms and is therefore naked from the waist up. The other pair of pyjamas is hanging from a roof beam in the corner of the room in an attempt to dry them. All because Caldicott clumsily dropped the other pair of pyjamas into the bowl of water, whilst having the embarrassing conversation with the maid earlier that evening.

Anna the Hotel Maid enters the bedroom; she has her coat on and is carrying a hat and what appears to be a dress. As she enters the room, a big grin appears on her face, amused at the sight of the two men in bed together, one of which is visibly naked from the waist up. Charters' immediate reaction is to wonder what on earth she is smiling at, but quickly realises that it may be due to his friend's semi-nakedness and puts his arm across in front of Caldicott in order to bring some respectability to the situation. The Maid continues into the room, to which the two Englishmen lean back, uncomfortable, not at being in bed together half dressed, but at being half dressed in the presence of a woman. Charters and Caldicott are very uncomfortable with this intrusion into their privacy.

In a feeble attempt to disguise his embarrassment, Charters starts whistling nonchalantly. Ignoring the two men sat side by side in the bed; Anna approaches them and bends down to pick up an octagonal hat box, which she knows is just under the edge of the bed. She places her hat into the box and replaces it under the bed, all under the watchful eyes of the two Englishmen. Still smiling, Anna goes across the room to the wardrobe where she hangs the dress and collects another item of clothing. Charters is still whistling as the maid leaves the room, although it is the same melody repeated over and over again.

Just as quickly as the door closes behind her and silence returns to the room, the maid quickly returns, this time without knocking. She is still smiling and says "Gute Nacht", leaves the room and closes the door behind her. Whilst not familiar with the local Bandrikan language they both know the translation as Goodnight. Charters gets out of bed just wearing his pyjama top, and says "Can't stand this ridiculous lack of privacy. I'm going to lock the door". The door in question has his dinner jacket hanging on the back of it, with a neatly folded white handkerchief in the top pocket. As he gets to the door, the jacket moves and once again the door opens to reveal Anna the maid standing there.

Anna the maid (Kathleen Tremaine) comes to collect her hat from beneath the bed that Charters and Caldicott have to share

Saying "hello" again, she enters, forcing Caldicott to step back in surprise and in the process he bangs his head on one of the room's several low beams. Charters looks on without making comment; he was already aware of the low beams, not just because he too had banged his head on one earlier in the evening, but also because he had made use of one earlier as a means of hanging his wet pyjamas on to dry.

Anna has another attempt at sorting out her clothes and puts some items into her chest of drawers. Just before she leaves the room, Charters moves closer to the door, silently hinting for decency sakes, that he wants her to leave as quickly as possible. He stands with his right hand on the roof beam, almost standing to attention as a sailor would when saluting a ship's captain coming aboard. She notices the less than subtle hint but makes no immediate rush to leave; whilst says Gute Nacht again, to the instant relief of Charters, she stoops to look at Charters' naked legs peeking out below his pyjama top.

Charters doesn't want to bang his head again as Anna (Kathleen Tremaine) the maid finally leaves the room.

The sight of the legs and Charters standing almost to attention brings out a big smile on the Maid's face before she finally leaves the room.

Charters knew that the maid found the whole situation very amusing, almost to the point of absurdity, as she struggled to stifle her laughter. The incident does not even bring a smile to Charter's face, though he is very, very embarrassed.

The train leaves Bandrika

The rest of the night is uneventful for the two Englishmen and the morning brings news that the train will finally be continuing on its journey out of Bandrika and onwards through Europe. Other people have also heard the news and are leaving the hotel straight onto the railway platform; in the background, a local musician and an accordion plays for tips from the tourists and provides a musical accompaniment to their departure. Amongst the people leaving the hotel are Charters and Caldicott. Both dressed in tweed overcoats to keep out the cold mountain air, they also wear; Charters has a trilby on whilst Caldicott wears a smart looking flat cap to match his overcoat. As they step onto the platform, Caldicott turns to Charters to say "I hope we get to Basle on time; we should catch the last part of the match".
They both look up at the clear blue sky; Charters, pleased with what he sees, replies "I hope the weather is like this in Manchester; perfect for the wicket for our fellows"; Caldicott nods in agreement. They board the train in the not unreasonable expectation, of a swift journey without any further delays.

Later that day, the train is well into its re-timetabled journey and Charters and Caldicott feel more relaxed with the comforting knowledge that they will be back in England in sufficient time for their appointment. The two Englishmen are in the restaurant carriage having afternoon tea. They have found a nice spot at the end of the car with their backs to the carriage wall and facing the front of the train. This is the best place to sit whilst travelling on long train journeys. Whilst it is a good spot in the sense that they can see where they are going, rather than looking at where they have just been, neither of them are looking out of the window. Instead they are concentrating on cricket, or rather talking about a game that they both love so dearly. In particular they are discussing a match that Charters had had the privilege of having seen.
"Nothing much about it, he wasn't out, that's all" says Charters, "if it wasn't for the umpire's blunder, he'd still be batting".

Caldicott offers a cigarette and his friend takes one from the proffered silver case. "What do you mean, I don't understand" asks Caldicott. "Look here, I'll show you the whole thing" replies Charters as he gets hold of the silver sugar bowl and empties the cubes from it to use as aids in his description of the critical part of the game.

Charters starts to explain in detail. Caldicott gets his lighter form his waistcoat pocket in order to light the two cigarettes. Charters now starts positioning the sugar cubes into how he considers the field of play was at the critical point
"Now then, here's Hammond" he says, "There's the bowler. There's the umpire". He thoughtfully takes the cigarette out of his mouth, taps Caldicott on the arm and says "Now, watch this very very carefully Caldicott. Grimmett was bowling".
Before he can continue, an elderly English lady sitting on the opposite side of the carriage a little further down asks "May I trouble you for the sugar please". The two Englishmen, disturbed from their table top game of cricket, look up. They see that it is Miss Froy, the elderly English lady from the hotel dining room the previous night. She is sitting with a young woman, who they immediately recognise as she was one of the three young women who arrived at the hotel. They recognised her because the group of women knew the Hotel manager and bagged not only the last available rooms, but also the last plates of food. Partly irritated by the presence of the young woman and partly annoyed by the interruption to their talk of cricket, Charters can't, or rather doesn't, understand what Miss Froy is saying and rather rudely asks "What?"
The elderly lady politely repeats her request "The sugar please".

Charters and Caldicott both understand the request now but are annoyed with this disruption to their play; they look at each other to indicate not only their disappointment but also their annoyance with the old lady. Reluctantly and with a bit of huffing, they collect the sugar cubes and replace them into the bowl.
The task grudgingly completed, Caldicott looks across to where Miss Froy is sitting and scowls at her, clearly showing that his annoyance has not subsided. Charters, like an indignant school boy, grudgingly complies with the polite request and picks up the replenished sugar bowl and walks across to where the two ladies are sitting. As he plonks

the bowl on the table and returns to his own seat, Miss Froy politely says "Thank you so much"

Caldicott is not happy that Charters use of sugar cubes to explain a game of cricket has been stopped

This is serious

Sometime later, Charters stands in the carriage corridor outside his compartment and knocks on the toilet door and whispers "Caldicott, its' Charters. Can I come in?"

The toilet door opens and a jacketless Caldicott walks into the corridor still drying his hands on a white towel. Charters asks "Do you know that girl we saw back at the hotel?" Nodding along the corridor he continues "She's back there, kicking up the devil of a fuss. She says she's lost her friend"
Sarcastically, Caldicott replies "Well she hasn't been in here old man".
"What if she threatens to stop the train?" asks Charters.
"Oh Lord!" exclaims Caldicott,

"If we miss our connection in Basle we'll never make Manchester in time" continues his friend.

Caldicott also realises the implications and adds "This is serious".

"Exactly" says Charters, "Let's hide in here" and gestures towards the toilet. Throughout the conversation Caldicott has been drying his hands; after such a good rub, they are now definitely dry. They both look around to make sure nobody sees them entering the toilet compartment together before closing the door behind them.

After some twenty minutes have passed, the two Englishmen consider that all the fuss will have died down and therefore any possibility of becoming embroiled in issues that they do want to become embroiled in will have disappeared. They quietly leave their hiding place, venturing out into the corridor in the hope that the crisis will have been averted. However, their feelings of safely avoiding any fuss are short lived. From behind them a young English woman says "There he is, that's the man". Charters turns to face his accuser and would be inquisitor and sees that it is the woman who stayed at the hotel with her two friends and who was also taking tea with Miss Froy in the dining car. Her name is Miss Iris Henderson and he sees that she is now accompanied by a young man.

The young man, addressing his question to Charters and Caldicott says "Oh, I say. I wonder if I could bother you. I wonder if you could help."

Caldicott is still putting his jacket on, so Charters comes to his friend's aid and sullenly responds "How?" He is annoyed at being found coming out of his hiding place and also of being accosted in this manner.

Miss Henderson, the young woman, asks "Well, I was having tea about an hour ago with an English Lady. You saw her didn't you?"

Charters doesn't like telling lies, but more importantly he doesn't want to miss the connection at Basle which in turn will see him missing the test match at Manchester. Nervously, he rubs his neck and replies "Well, I don't know. I mean, I was talking to my friend, wasn't I" as he looks to Caldicott for support.

Caldicott joins in the deception but he also does not want to lie, "Indubitably" he says.

Miss Henderson continues with her questioning "Yes, but you were sitting at the next table. She came and borrowed the sugar. You must remember?"

"Oh yes, I remember passing the sugar" says Charters.

Now very excited, she loudly demands "Well, you saw her?"

Not only is Charters uncomfortable around screeching women, he also does not appreciate being shouted at by one. Nor is he particularly fond of being dictated to about what he did or did not see. His wrath ignited, he raises his voice "I repeat, we were in deep conversation. We were discussing cricket."

Well, I don't see how a thing like cricket can make you forget seeing people?" she says

Charters is flabbergasted at this unacceptable comment on top of what has just been said and retorts "Oh, don't you? Well if that's your attitude, obviously there's nothing more to say. Come Caldicott"

Through much of this conversation, Caldicott has been adjusting the wrist strap of his watch, in between nervous glances at Charters and the young couple and has said nothing to either compound or defuse the conversation. He is torn between wanting Charters to tell the truth, uncomfortable as he is with lying, but also dearly not wanting their journey to be delayed any further. His desire for the journey to continue uninterrupted wins the day and he remains silent on whether r not they saw the old lady – 'bad form' be damned he thinks.

Still exasperated with the young couple, Charters finally says "Thing like cricket" with a tone of disgust in his voice and he and Caldicott walk down the train corridor away from the young couple. They clearly have no concept of the reverence placed on the game of cricket by the two Englishmen; a reverence, in their view that should be shared by all, particularly fellow Englishmen (and women for that matter).

The train continues its journey northwards after making a timetabled stop at Dravka and also an emergency stop, which not only had the effect of jolting people from their seats and moments of slumber but also delayed the train for ten minutes while the engine driver and his colleagues make the necessary safety checks. The speedy resumption in the journey gives Charters and Caldicott renewed hope that they will be back in time to catch the Test Match in Manchester

Iris Henderson (Margaret Lockwood) and Gilbert (Michael Redgrave) catch Charters and Caldicott as they come out of the toilet and ask them about the missing lady.

All is well in the world, at least in the world occupied by Charters and Caldicott. They are on their way to the third Ashes Test match in Manchester between England and Australia. That is, if there are no further delays to their journey. Charters has his feet resting on the seat opposite, and in a relaxed but thoughtful mood smokes his pipe, puffing away. Opposite him, sits his friend, or rather lounging along the seat with his back to the window, trying to read a newspaper. Unfortunately the newspaper contains not one word of English and Caldicott speaks only English; he is perplexed that anybody would want to speak, never mind read, another language. Notwithstanding this minor inconsistency, he nevertheless struggles on trying to make some sense from the confusion of foreign words mangled as though they mean something of importance

Charters and Caldicott are pleased that their train journey has resumed after the unwanted emergency stop.

Charters, thinking out loud, says "Huh, ten minutes delayed. Thanks to that foolish girl. If she gets up to any more of her tricks, we'll be too late for the last day of the match".

"I suppose you couldn't put it to her in some way?" queries Caldicott. Realising that he has been speaking out loud and not quite hearing what Caldicott has just said, Charters asks "What?"

Caldicott continues "Well, people just don't vanish and so forth" and returns to reading or trying to read his newspaper.

Charters picks up a book but rather than read it he thoughtfully places it on his knee and says "She has".

"What?" says Caldicott.

"Vanished" replies his friend.

"Who?" says Caldicott, forgetting the earlier conversation with the young lady and the events and conversations that have since followed.

"The old dame" says Charters.

Caldicott agrees "yes".

"Well?" questions Charters.

Caldicott breaks the near mono-syllabic conversation with "Well how could she?"
Charters continues in the style of conversation that is typical of Englishmen when they are clearly busy doing something far more riveting than trying to have a conversation and says "What?"

Also reverting back to the more natural style of conversation, Caldicott replies "Vanish".
Shaking his head, Charters replies "I don't know".
"That just explains my point. People just don't disappear" says Caldicott.
Not sure that it does explain a point, Charters is reminded of something he saw at a bazaar on one of their earlier trips and says "It's done in India". "What?" asks Caldicott.
"The rope trick" replies Charters.
Clearly not convinced about the merits of the Indian rope trick, Caldicott points out "Oh that, it never comes out in a photograph"

They both continue trying to read, Charters has his book and Caldicott his newspaper; he reads or rather tries to read the newspaper despite the fact that it does not have a single word of English in it.

The old girl turned up

Later that day, the two English friends are in the dining car; Charters is drinking brandy whilst Caldicott is enjoying the pleasures of a cigar. They are both soon distracted from their pleasures as they see Miss Henderson accompanied by her friend Gilbert.
"There's that girl again" whispers Charters.
"Seems to have recovered; lucky it blew over" replies Caldicott glancing disdainfully at her. Hopeful that the whole matter may have been resolved and that there will be no further delays in their pilgrimage to Manchester and the test match, they both shrug and return to their respective pleasures of brandy and cigars. Their feelings of hope are short-lived as they see the young woman with her friend, the young Englishman, talking to a foreign looking gentleman. "She's off again" says Charters.
"Hope she doesn't create another scene. It will only delay us getting back in time if she does" adds Caldicott.

40

The train makes its scheduled stop at Morsken, and Charters and Caldicott are in the dining car again; tea time for the English travellers. As it is tea time, the dining car, like any other dining room in the world at this particularly important time, plays host to English people only. Tea time for the English is a very important part of the day, a time of day not to be missed for those who have any sense of proportion. The dining car is alive with the clinking of silver spoons and fine bone china as the young English couple enter, accompanied by Miss Froy, the old lady that had supposedly disappeared.

"There, the old girl turned up" points out Charters.

Caldicott turns to look and replies "I told you there was a lot of fuss about nothing. A bolt must have jammed"

Gilbert, the young Englishman, is standing at the end of the dining car and loudly addresses everybody there. Solemnly he says "I've got something to say. Will you all please listen? An attempt has been made to abduct this lady by force. I believe that the people who did it are going to try again"

An older Englishman further down the dining car retorts angrily "What the devil is the fellow dribbling about"

The young Englishman walks along the carriage passing Charters and Caldicott and says to the questioning man "Well if you don't believe me, look out of the window. This train has been diverted onto a branch line"

Again the older Englishman questions him by snapping "What on earth are you talking about. Abductions, Diverted trains?"

"We are telling you the truth" hysterically shouts Miss Henderson seeing that her fellow passengers still do not believe her.

The older Englishman continues with his pompous diatribe and says "I'm not the least bit interested. You've annoyed us enough with your ridiculous story".

Uncomfortably for the two Englishmen, Charters and Caldicott are caught in the centre of the argument. Reserved as they are, this is not the sort of thing they would choose to have any part in, but everybody seems to have gathered around their table where they remain seated.

In any other circumstance, they would have excused themselves and left the others to continue with the heated discussion, whilst they resumed their afternoon tea somewhere that had an atmosphere with more decorum.

41

Feeling the need to calm things down and prevent the heated debate from developing into a full blown argument, Charters says "My dear chap, you must have got hold of the wrong end of the stick somewhere"

Caldicott follows his friends lead by calmly adding "Yes, things like that just don't happen"

Miss Froy, not looking any worse the wear for having supposedly disappeared, responds to Charters' and Caldicott's voices of reason and says "We're not in England now".

Caldicott retorts "I don't see what difference that makes".

Iris Henderson leans over the table where Charters and Caldicott are sitting and exclaims shrilly "We're stopping". Sure enough the train slows to a halt, to the group of English travellers looking out the window; it looks like they have stopped in the middle of some woods as all they can see in any direction are trees and nothing else.

Except something else can be seen; Gilbert, the young Englishman says "See those cars? They are here to take Miss Froy away"

Caldicott retorts "nonsense" and looks out of the window to see two cars parked on a track in the woods. Standing next to the cars are a group of soldiers in dark uniforms. As he looks, he sees two of the soldiers moving off from the main group and heading towards the train, which he points out to the people stood behind him.

Miss Henderson immediately puts her arms around Miss Froy as if to protect her; Gilbert automatically does the same; both wearing very worried expressions on their faces.

We Are British subjects

Caldicott tries to offer a simple explanation "The cars have obviously come to pick them up".

"In that case, why go to the trouble of uncoupling the train and diverting it?" says Gilbert.

Looking very concerned now, both Charters and Caldicott immediately turn around, Charters asks "Uncoupling?"

The young Englishman replies "There's nothing left of the train behind the sleeping car".

Caldicott says "There must be, our bags are in the First Class carriage".

Charters nods in agreement.

"Not any longer. Like to come and look?" replies the young Englishman.

Caldicott stands to go and look but before he leaves the carriage he says "If this is a practical joke, I won't take it very kindly". As he opens the door connecting with the next carriage, he is startled by the sight of a nun falling through the doorway towards him; she has been bound and gagged.

Gilbert and Caldicott just manage to catch her before she hits the floor and steady her into a standing position. "Good Lord" says Caldicott. Between them they half walk and half carry her into the dining car and sit her down in Caldicott's former place opposite Charters. Not quite sure what to do in a situation, unusual as this, Charters stands, napkin in hand, in unfamiliar and uncomfortable territory.

"Bring some of that brandy" says Miss Henderson helpfully as the other passengers fuss around the nun.

"Charters turns to his friend, nervously and quietly says ""You don't suppose that there's something in this, err, fellow's story, Caldicott? Do you?"

Caldicott responds "It seems a bit queer"

"Well after all, people don't go around tying up nuns" adds Charters.

The nun has a drink of the brandy that was fetched for her, splutters and silently sighs a big thank you.

The silence is sharply interrupted by Miss Henderson shrieking "Someone's coming" as she glances out of the carriage window to the woods beyond.

All the passengers follow her lead and look out of the window to see a soldier, looking up at the train from a short distance away. From the way he is dressed it is clear to all that he is an army officer, with his military great coat and an officer's cap. They don't have long to watch him as he starts moving through the woods and swiftly moves out of sight to the right of the train; they glimpse him rushing from bush to bush, trying not to be seen.

The older Englishman, who had just introduced his companion and himself as Mr and Mrs Todhunter, pompously says "They can't possibly do anything to us, we are British subjects".

Before anybody has an opportunity to join in the conversation, the Army Officer who was last seen in the woods now enters through the door into to the dining car. Startled, everybody turns to see the Officer stand to attention to salute them. All, that is, except for the nun and the young Englishman who are busily untying the ropes that bind her feet and hands.

"I have come to offer the most sincere apologies" says the Officer. "An extremely serious incident has occurred. An attempt has been made to interfere with passengers on this train. Fortunately it was brought to the notice of the authorities". He stops speaking as he notes the nun whispering something to the young Englishman but quickly continues. "And if you would be good enough to accompany me to Morsken, I will inform the British embassy at once. Ladies and Gentlemen, the cars are at your disposal". He finishes by saluting to the on looking travellers.

Caldicott is the first to speak saying "We are very grateful. Lucky that some of you fellows understand English".
The Officer replies "Well I was at Oxford".
"Oh really" says Charters, "so was I. What year?"
At this point, Gilbert stands up from where he has been attending to the nun and says "Hold on. This woman seems to be trying to say something. I don't understand the language. It may be important. Would you" and continues by nodding to the nun sitting on the floor next to him.
The officer obliges and bends to speak to the nun. To the shock and disbelieve of the other passengers, Gilbert immediately springs into action as his unannounced plan unfolds. He picks up a chair and smashes it as hard as he can on the Officers head, successfully knocking him unconscious and says "That's fixed him".
Somewhat taken aback, the others watch as the events quickly unfold. However, Caldicott, with a great deal of calmness knowingly says "He's only stunned".

After the initial shock, Charters springs to his senses and realises what the young Englishman has just done; he snaps "What the blazes did you go that for?"
Being facetious, Gilbert replies "Well I was at Cambridge"
Caldicott, not amused with the sarcastic comment retorts "What has that got to do with it? You heard what he said, didn't you?"
Gilbert nods towards the nun and explains "I heard what she said. It was a trick to get us off the train.

44

Listening to what has been said, Mr Todhunter says "I don't believe it. The man's explanation was quite satisfactory"

After some thinking Charters steps forward and says "A thing like this might cause a war. I'm going outside to tell them what has occurred and try to apologise and put the matter right". From the faces of the other passengers there is a mixed showing of agreement and apprehension.

Charters goes to leave the train and try and find a diplomatic solution to the situation that appears to be getting worse minute by minute. At the back of his mind is the dark thought that he and Caldicott might not make it back to England in time to catch the test match to be played at Manchester. Slowly, he opens the door of the carriage and steadies himself before trying to climb down the steps into the woods to find somebody in charge to speak to. Before he gets very far, he hears a sound that sounds very much like the crack of a gun; at the same time he feels a sharp pain in his left hand. He knows what the noise was and worryingly looks at his hand and finds that his fears are confirmed; he has been shot. Looking in the direction where he heard the crack of the gun he sees a number of soldiers crouching or standing but all pointing either rifles or pistols at the railway carriage, or more worryingly at him. He quickly retreats back into the shadows of the carriage and closes the door behind him.

Re-entering the dining compartment, he does not want any fuss making of the incident and nonchalantly shows his bloodied hand to the other passengers. They also heard the shot and fearing the worse outcome rush to Charters and inspect his hand.

Coolly, Charters turns to Gilbert; nodding his head he says "You were right".

Charters turns to Caldicott who his holding the injured hand in the way that a doctor would, whilst also looking through the window at the soldiers. Charters, polite as ever says "Do you mind", and helps himself to the hanky sitting neatly in Caldicott's top pocket.

Caldicott nods his approval whilst continuing to stare at the events in the woods.

It doesn't take long for his fellow passengers to tie a neat bandage around Charters' hand but it seems an eternity for those continuing to look through the window at the waiting soldiers. Charters, following the gaze of the others, sees that the soldiers are gathered back at the cars says "Looks as if they mean business".

To which, Gilbert replies in agreement "I'm afraid so"

Todhunter, the older Englishman adds "Well they can't do anything. It would mean an international situation"

Knowingly, Miss Froy says "It has happened before"

Everybody is silent.

Out in the woods, an elderly man, who Charters recognises as a passenger from the train, approaches the carriage accompanied by a group of soldiers.

Miss Henderson exclaims loudly "They're coming".

The nun shouts "Don't let them in. They will murder us". Everybody looks aghast at the nun who continues saying "They daren't let us go now".

Gilbert looks out of the window and sees that some sort of defensive action is required and quickly; something has to be done. He rushes over to the still unconscious Officer lying on the floor and takes his gun out of his holster. Checking to see that it is loaded, he quickly moves back to his vantage point and opens the window.

In the woods the man and the three soldiers come to a standstill a short distance from the carriage. Addressing the passengers sheltering in the train carriage, the man shouts "I order you to surrender at once". Confidently, the young Englishman replies "Nothing doing. Come any nearer and I'll fire" and points the pistol through the open window.

The old man with the soldiers continues to make his demands of the English passengers, "I warn you" before swiftly moving out of the line of fire behind a bush.

Without hesitating, Gilbert fires the pistol and with his first shot hits one of the three soldiers who were approaching the train.

Turning to address his fellow passengers, he says "You'd better take cover. It will start any minute now." Following his suggestion, the passengers swiftly go to take cover but find little opportunity in a dining car with large windows down both sides of the carriage.

Charters and Caldicott are sheltering near the young Englishman, Caldicott says "A nasty jam this, I don't like the look of it".

46

Charters tries to be more positive about the situation and asks "Got enough ammunition?"

Pointing to the still unconscious Officer, Gilbert replies "Whole pouch full".

Charters nods and says "Good".

Caldicott sees that some of the passengers are not sheltering very well, particularly Todhunter. He indicates with his arm and shouts to him "Duck down you".

Not happy about how the situation is developing into a major incident, he snarls back "I'm not going to fight. It's madness".

His wife, Mrs Todhunter, worried about his safety, says to him "It will be safer to protest down here". Pompously, he does not want to be seen not in charge of events and he resists her attempt to pull him down to the floor. He remains half standing, half crouching, desperately trying to find a solution to the events unfolding before him, a solution that more befits his view of the world.

As the travellers look through the window they see soldiers moving from behind the parked cars towards nearby bushes. Gilbert points this out to the others and says "Hello. They are trying to work round to the other side"

Todhunter is now fully standing and snarls to the others "You are behaving like a pack of fools. What chance have we got against a lot of armed men?"

In response Caldicott reasons "You heard what the Mother Superior said? If we surrender now we are in for it."

The battle between the occupants of the solitary railway carriage and the soldiers in the woods continues. Gilbert manages to wound two of the soldiers creeping towards the train, oblivious to the heated discussions going on behind him. In response to their colleague's plight, the soldiers fire a rally of shots at the railway carriage hitting some of the windows and smashing the glass. One shot is fired through an open window and smashes into a vase of flowers on one of the tables, smashing it into smithereens and sending splashes of water and pot debris across the carriage.

They are in a tight spot, with the likely outcome looking very grim. Uncertain whether or not they will be able to resume their journey, Caldicott says to Charters "We'll never get to the match now". Unsure what to do next, and looking for some sort of answer, he looks around to survey the situation and sees the Todhunter couple arguing at one of the carriage.

She says "Give it to me, give it to me"

Todhunter is resisting her demands "No, no, no"

All in all, Caldicott can see that she is getting hysterical whilst her husband is getting more adamant and vociferous in refusing her demands. Not wanting to interfere between a married couple. Seeing that it might be better to step in, Caldicott manages to crawl over to the quarrelling couple, all the while mindful of the bullets being fired through the windows into the carriage. "What's going on here" he asks.

She replies "He's got a gun and he won't use it" accusingly.

"What's the idea?" asks Caldicott.

Todhunter coldly replies "I won't be party to this sort of thing. I don't believe in fighting".

Pacifist eh?" says Caldicott, clearly disgusted with the attitude of his fellow countryman in a time of crisis. "It won't work old boy. The Christians tried it and got thrown to the lions. Come on, hand it over." She grabs the gun off her cowardly companion and crawls to the window where Caldicott had just come from with the intention of using it herself.

At the window, the English woman stands and points the gun out of the window and says to Caldicott who had crawled back with her "I'm not afraid to use it".

I'm probably more used to it" says Caldicott "I once won a box of cigars"

Overhearing the conversation between Caldicott and the woman, Charters interrupts "He's talking rot. He's a damn good shot".

Caldicott takes the gun from the woman and starts shooting out through the window, "Hope the old hand hasn't lost its cunning. Still I'm inclined to believe that there's some rational explanation to all this". A couple of shots later, Caldicott adds "Rotten shot; I only knocked his hat off"

Further along the carriage, Miss Froy the elderly English lady asks Gilbert "Would you mind if I talk to you for a minute?"

Clearly torn between keeping the soldiers at bay and not wanting to dismiss Miss Froy, he asks "What, now?"

"Yes, sorry. Please forgive me but it is very important" says Miss Froy. Gilbert passes the gun to Charters and asks "Here, hang onto this for a minute, will you?"
Charters dutifully takes the gun, saying "All right. I'll hold the fort for you"

"I think it's safe along here" says Miss Froy leading the way to where she wants a quite word with the young man. You'll come too, won't you?" she says to Miss Henderson.
As they move away from the line of fire, Gilbert notices that Miss Froy is still standing and finds the necessity to put his hand on her back saying "Keep your head down".

Back at the window, both Charters and Caldicott are firing away at the soldiers. In a short break in the shooting, Caldicott has a quick look around and sees Miss Froy singing or humming to the young English couple. Nodding at the group of three huddled in the corner he says to Charters "Hello, looks like the old woman has gone off her rocker"

At the other end of the carriage, Todhunter hears what Caldicott has just said about Miss Froy and blurts out "I shouldn't wonder. Why don't you face it, those swine will go on until they kill us?"
Caldicott looks at him with great disdain and sees no need to say anything to such a cowardly response. He turns and carries on surveying the situation in the woods.
Mrs Todhunter feels the need to respond to her cowardly companion, tiring of his pathetic behaviour, "For goodness sake, shut up Eric", she hysterically says, with equal measures of anger and shame.

Caldicott fires his last shot at the soldiers and turns to the English woman and says "Well that's the end of my twelve" and puts the gun down on the adjacent table.
At the next window, Charters is also crouching and shooting replies "There's not much left here either"

Miss Froy has now stopped humming the tune to the young couple and Gilbert crawls back over to Charters. "We've only got one chance now" the young man says "We've got to get this train going".

An astonished Charters looks at him, but before he has time to say anything he continues "Go back to the main line and try and cross the frontier".

Caldicott, now standing at the end of the carriage with Todhunter, drily replies "A bit of a tall order isn't it? These driver fellows are not likely to do as you tell them, you know"

Gilbert crawls over to where Caldicott is standing and picks up the gun, the empty gun! "We'll bluff them with this" he says. "Who's coming?"

"You can count on me" replies Caldicott thinking that the plan has some merit.

Charters, who has been carefully listening, whilst continuing to shoot, adds, "Me too!" He is of the view that wherever his friend goes, then he goes too.

The young Englishman shakes his head in disagreement and says "Oh, we can't all go. You stay here and carry on" directing his comment to Charters. "If we have any luck, we'll stop the train when we reach the points and you'll jump out and switch them over", grinning at Charters, he opens the door of the carriage.

"Okay" says Charters pleased with his role in the escape plan

Todhunter, shouts "You idiots. You are just inviting death"
Not bothering to reply, Caldicott and Gilbert man leave the compartment

Todhunter continues with his cowardly tirade, but directing his comments at no one in particular saying "I've had enough. Just because I've the sense to try and avoid being murdered, I'm accused of being a pacifist. Turning to his companion he continues "Alright, I'd rather be called a rat than die like one".

Addressing everybody in the carriage now, he continues with his speech "Think thoroughly will you? If we give ourselves up, they daren't murder us in cold blood. They're bound to give us a trial". Shouting him down, his lady companion says "Stop gibbering Eric. Nobody's listening to you".

Hurt by this cutting remark he adds "Very well. You go your way, I'll go mine". Taking his white handkerchief from his jacket pocket he makes his way to leave the dining car and to foolishly surrender.

"Hey, where are you off to?" shouts Charters.

Todhunter replies "I know what I'm about. I am doing the only sensible thing", waving his white handkerchief he walks out of the door.

"Oh let the fellow go if he wants to" says Charters, clearly disgusted with the man's cowardly behaviour.

Charters watches the cowardly Todhunter climbs down the steps from the carriage, waving his white handkerchief. He sees him walk two or three steps from the railway carriage before a gunshot loudly rings out. The single shot hits Todhunter and forces him to drop to the floor. The two English women join Charters at the window; from where they stand they see Todhunter still waving his white handkerchief whilst lying bloodied on the grass. It isn't long before the feeble waving stops; at that point they know that he is dead. The superior pomposity, the cowardly behaviour and his feeble attempt to surrender achieved nothing.

Upset at the killing of Todhunter, cowardly though he was, Charters bites his lip and fires a couple of shots into the woods partly out of anger at the murder of a fellow Englishman and partly because he is the only man in the carriage with the responsibility of protecting the three English women.

Mrs Todhunter is obviously distraught at his death and buries her face into her hands. Miss Henderson tries to comfort her but no words of comfort will quench her pain and sorrow. Hysterically she half sobs half scream "Don't. Please. Why aren't we going? They said we were going. Why aren't we?"

Just as frightened, the young woman sobs "If only he can get us away now; he must."

Breaching his gun, Charters looks down at it and quietly says "Only one left. I'll keep that for a sitter" and snaps shut the gun.

Miss Henderson, looking through the window, notices movement and shouts "They are moving away from the cars and coming towards us".

"It's a pity that we haven't a few more rounds" replies Charters forlornly, desperate at the seemingly dire situation they now face.

Iris (Margaret Lockwood) and 'Mrs' Todhunter (Linden Travers) look on as Charters uses the last of the ammunition.

The startling news of the approaching enemy strangely brings a little composure to the older English woman despite her tragic loss. She says "Its' funny. I told my husband when I left him that I wouldn't see him again". The others are perplexed and unsure of the meaning of what she has just said; they thought that Todhunter was her husband; what did she mean when she said that "she left him?" not knowing exactly what to say, the others say nothing.

The feeling of hysteria passes from the older woman to the younger one, who screams out her friends name "Gilbert, Gilbert!"

Charters is more comfortable dealing with an armed enemy than an hysterical woman, and not knowing how to react in these emotional situations; he does what any other Englishman would do. Sighing, he walks away from the window and leaves the women to their hysteria.

Suddenly the train jolts. The four remaining passengers of Charters, the nun and the two English women are all equally jolted into silence. Steadying himself, Charters exclaims "By golly, we're off!"

Slowly the train moves and the passengers rush to the windows to see the soldiers' running back to their cars.

Meanwhile, in the engine compartment, Caldicott and Gilbert are standing over the engine driver and his mate. The younger of the two Englishmen is holding the gun and says to the driver's mate "Go on. Keep going" as he is forced to shovel coal into the engine's boiler. Suddenly a shot rings out and the engine driver slumps to the floor clutching his stomach. A second shot sees the driver's mate also hit who stumbles backwards out of the moving engine onto the track side. The two people who could control the train engine have been shot dead

Caldicott and Gilbert take a moment to look at the controls of the now driverless engine. Shouting to be heard over the deafening roar of the engine, Caldicott says "I say, do you know how to control this thing?" The young man replies "I watched the fellow start it. Anyway, I know something about it. I once drove a miniature engine on the Dymchurch Line"
"Oh good, I'll look out for the points" shouts Caldicott relieved to hear that one of them can work the controls that will take them to safety.
Caldicott stands at the edge of the footplate and looks along the track for the points; as he does, he spots the soldiers chasing the train in their cars.

Charters also sees the cars chasing them and says to the three ladies with him in the dining car "The blighters are chasing us. Look!"
"We can't have far to go" says Miss Henderson in desperation.
Charters answers "It's time for my little job changing the points. Then we shall be in neutral territory".

Whilst looking through the window for the points that he needs to change, he doesn't see the Officer regain consciousness on the floor of the carriage. Neither does he see him take the gun off the table and check to see whether or not it is loaded.. Clicking the gun shut, the Officer says "That will not be necessary". Startled, Charters and his fellow passengers turn round to see the Officer standing and pointing the gun at them. "I am sorry, but the points as you call them will not be changed over" says the Officer. In charge of the situation and his

53

prisoners once more, he says "Please be seated and the other passengers all sit down".

Back on the engine footplate, Caldicott sees the points and says to Gilbert "There they are, just ahead of us. Do you think you can stop it?"

"Hope so" he replies.

Meanwhile in the dining car, the Officer says to the passengers "Keep still until my friends arrive. Anyone move, I'm afraid I'll have to shoot them".

The Officer directs his comments at Charters and the two English women; but he doesn't see the nun who is sitting on a chair behind him. She is still recovering from her earlier ordeal of being bound and gagged. Silently, she stands up and puts one finger to her mouth to indicate to the other passengers that they should keep quiet about her presence.

Latching onto the Nun's plan, Miss Henderson stands and says to the officer "There's just one thing you don't know Captain. There's only one bullet left in that gun and if you shoot me you'll give the others a chance. You are rather in a difficult position aren't you?"

Whilst the Officer is distracted, the nun silently moves to the end of the carriage and removes the bandage wrapped around her head in order that she can see better to leave the carriage.

Being a soldier, the Officer believes he knows how to handle situations like this and maintain control. He stands his ground and firmly demands "Sit down please".

Seeing that the nun has left the carriage, Miss Henderson agrees, "All right" she says, smiling at the Officer and obediently sits.

"Where the deuce is Charters" asks Caldicott standing beside Gilbert on the engine footplate. The train has been at a standstill for what seems like ages and there is no sight of Charters; the points need to be changed if they are to have any chance of escaping into neutral territory.

Caldicott and Gilbert (Michael Redgrave) look for the points

At the back of the remaining short length of train, the nun climbs down from the carriage and runs to the points, to do what Charters is being prevented from doing. Arriving at the points, the car with the pursuing soldiers pulls up close by and soldiers leap out to start firing shots at the nun. Stiff as the points are, with shots ringing around her, the nun nevertheless manages to change the points and heads back to the train.
Caldicott sees what is happening and shouts to this companion on the footplate "Go ahead. She's done it"
Slowly but surely, Gilbert works the controls and the train starts moving again; they quickly draw level with the nun and under fire from the pursuing soldiers they help her to get onto the engine plate. Just as she stands she lets out a large groan as a gunshot hits her, "It's alright, it's just my leg" she says.

As the train crosses the border, Gilbert pulls the engine whistle. Caldicott notices him whistling a familiar tune.
"Well old boy", he says, "I'm glad that's all over. Aren't you? Heaven knows what the government will say about it"

"Nothing at all; they'll hush it all up" replies the young man.

As the train picks up speed, Caldicott feels the need to steady himself and puts his hand out to find something to hold onto. Unfortunately, he grabs hold of the whistle pull and a loud screeching whistle drowns out any further conversation.

"What?" shouts Caldicott.

"Take your hand off that thing" says the young man "I'm trying to remember a tune"

Not sure what the young man is on about, Caldicott smiles and asks "Remembering a tune?"

Gilbert doesn't reply but starts to whistle the tune again.

The Test Match

Back in England, the trans-European train finally pulls into London and stops on Platform 7. Charters and Caldicott hurriedly alight and quickly walk along the platform rushing to get their connection. They have a copy of Bradshaw's rail guide with them and having studied it carefully, they know exactly what train to catch. "Ample time to catch the 6:50 to Manchester after all" says Charters.

To which, Caldicott checks his watch, before looking up to see where he is going

Within seconds, they both stop dead in their tracks as they see something written on a sign that causes them great alarm. The sign in question is a newspaper headline board being walked along the platform by a boy. It is the wording on the sign that specifically catches the traveller's eyes; it reads in capitals TEST MATCH ABANDONED FLOODS.

It is disastrous; how could this have happened? Words failing them, shocked and downhearted, they stand there for what seems like an eternity. All the trouble they have taken to ensure that they arrived back in time for the match has been to no avail. All the hardships that they have endured fade into insignificance compared to the loss of an enjoyable day watching England play cricket.

Charters and Caldicott find out about the Test Match.

Night Train to Munich

They haven't got a Punch, old man

Charters and Caldicott are once again on their travels. Taking a break from work, they have been touring distant parts of Europe, but are now looking forward to returning to England to watch an eagerly anticipated Cricket Test match. It is 3rd September 1939 and unbeknown to the two English travellers, the Europe that they know will be in a far more perilous state by the end of their journey, than it is before they set out. Already divisions and alliances amongst European countries are already being forged partly through political manoeuvring, but mostly through the use of military might.

They are at the main railway station in Prague, Czechoslovakia waiting for the train that will take them on the next leg of their annual travel around Europe. Munich is their destination. Charters is standing at the small kiosk on the platform browsing through the newspapers and magazines to find something to read during the impending train journey. Not seeing what he is looking for he asks the lady behind the magazine racks if she has the magazine, "Have you got a copy of this week's Punch?"
Not understanding a word of English she doesn't know what she has just been asked and replies "qe?"

Charters approach when speaking to foreigners who don't understand English is to speak very clearly, in short sentences and loud; so he tries again. "Punch; English magazine; Very humorous. You must have a copy." all in his best loud English especially reserved for speaking with foreigners. Whilst familiar with how English people speak to her on a daily basis at her news stand, she has never quite fathomed what they are trying to say; this particular English man is no exception and she shakes her head as a means of indicating that she doesn't understand.

Charters considers that she has understood him and is indicating no in answer; after all, everybody must understand English. He turns away from the kiosk and looks to the platform edge where the train to Munich is waiting. It will be another fifteen minutes before the train

59

leaves, so Charters had agreed to get some reading material for Caldicott and himself. He sees Caldicott leaning out of the open window of the carriage compartment and shouts to him "They haven't got a Punch old man!"

"Hasn't she?" Caldicott replies. "Oh, sold out I suppose".

"They've got old La Vie, old boy" Charters explains.

"La Vie Parisienne?, oh alright. Don't bother about a Punch" says Caldicott.

Charters turns back to the newspaper kiosk to complete his purchases, which includes a book for him that he has heard of; he buys a copy of Mein Kampf.

Charters asks for a copy of Punch magazine

Back in the compartment, Caldicott turns from his conversation with Charters at the window in order to take his seat and get comfortable. As he turns, he sees with a shock, that there are no other passengers. A moment ago, when he last looked, the compartment was almost full with other passengers. Now, apart from him, it is empty. He scans the compartment for an explanation, seeing none he walks to the door and looks up and down the corridor to see where everybody has gone.

None the wiser he puts his hat on the parcel shelf and sits down. Clearly perplexed, he pops his pipe into his mouth and gives the matter some thought. Moments later, Charters arrives with the newspapers; like his friend, he also enjoys smoking his pipe. Noticing that the compartment is now devoid of passengers, he enquires with a "oh?" "Everybody has hopped it" explains Caldicott.

Charters puts the newspapers down on his seat directly opposite Caldicott to remove his overcoat and put it on the parcel shelf. "Yes, must have got onto the wrong train I expect" he adds.

Clearly pleased with the surprising departure of the other passengers, Caldicott suggests "We can have a side each to ourselves now" and taking advantage of the opportunity he leans back against the side of the compartment and puts his feet up on the seat. Charters does likewise and both sit smoking their pipes enjoying their newly found space.

Caldicott shuffles in his seat and turns to look through the window in order to get a better view of the comings and goings on the platform. After all, he will have plenty of time to read his magazine on the journey to Munich and he decides to make better use of his time whilst there is something of interest to look at. Charters removes his hat in order to make himself more comfortable for the long journey. Leaning over he picks up the hardback book that he has just bought. "I bought a copy of Mein Kampf. You never know, it might shed a spot of light on all this 'how do you do'. Ever read it?" he asks.

"Never had the time" replies his friend.

"I understand that they give a copy to all the bridal couples over here" says Charters.

Without any hint of condescension, Caldicott corrects his friend misconception "Oh, I don't think it's that sort of book old man".

This causes Charters some confusion as he is unsure about what his friend thinks the book is about, but before he has the opportunity to enquire further, the compartment door opens and his attention is diverted.

There in the doorway, they see the train guard glaring at them. "Why are you still here?" he angrily shouts.

"Eh?" says Charters, looking up at the guard, as he puts down the copy of Mein Kampf.

It might shed a spot of light on all this 'how do you do' says Charters.

The guard angrily continues "You must find other place at once". Taking their feet of the seats, Charters and Caldicott both stand; "We have first class tickets you know" explains Caldicott. Standing behind the train guard, Charters notices the two German soldiers but not thinking too much of it, he says nothing.

"Outside please; this compartment has been commandeered by the authorities" continues the guard with his orders.

Charters has seen this sort of bullying officious behaviour before and has never been impressed by it nor feels obliged to do what he is being told to do; rather, he considers it his duty to take a stand, object to the instructions and generally respond with the same level of contempt. Not to be pushed around by officialdom, Charters retorts "That is beside the point"

"Yes" adds Caldicott in total agreement with his friend, "we are British subjects".

Charters agrees, "Yes" he says and stands directly in front of the guard and gets his passport out of his pocket in order to prove his Brutishness. "Look here" he adds, opening his passport and reads

from it, "We, Edward Frederick Lindley, Viscount Halifax, His Majesty's Principal Secretary of State etc, requests all Whom it may concern to allow the bearer to pass freely without let or hindrance and to afford him or her". Before he can complete reading the instruction from the British Government written in his passport, the guard, quite rudely, snatches it from him and snaps it firmly shut.
Swiftly giving it back to Charters he snaps "Outside"

Charters is furious at the guard's rudeness and impertinence. Not intimidated by the ridiculous posturing of the train guard, Charters looks him up and down; he decides not to bother retaliating with angry words but to sit down as a perverse, but English way, of standing his ground. Looking left and right at the two seated Englishmen who are showing their determination not to be moved, the train guard leaves the compartment. As he leaves, he nods to the two soldiers quietly standing outside in the corridor.

Feeling and looking very satisfied with themselves having seen off the impudent and officious train guard, Charters and Caldicott remain seated. Charters silently reads his passport again, taking great pride in the power and meaning of the words of the British Government and how he used them to stand his ground. Caldicott is also silently revelling in this small victory over the foreigner and enjoys a satisfying puff on his pipe; he is very impressed by his friend's tactics.

Moments later, Charters, having reread the passport several times, looks up, to see two soldiers standing menacingly in front of him. Caldicott is looking the other way through the carriage window and also hasn't noticed the soldiers, so he uses his passport to get his attention by tapping his friend's knee with it.
Turning round, Caldicott sees the soldiers for the first time and studiously looks them up and down, taking in their scowling faces. Puffing on his pipe, as he contemplates what their next move should, he calmly says to Charters "No good arguing I suppose?"
"Apparently not" replies Charters "A waste of time all this bilge in the passport", looking disappointingly at the open passport in his hand. The words did not have the effect that he was hoping for.
Together they realise that their victory was short lived stand and both stand to remove their luggage from the parcel shelves above where they were sitting.

We are British subjects' says Caldicott.

As they ready themselves to leave, the train guard returns accompanied with more soldiers; seeing that Charters and Caldicott are still there he snaps "Outside. Come along, hurry".

Before they have the opportunity to follow the instructions so impudently put to them, a man and young woman enter the compartment. Caldicott looks closely at the man and thinks that he knows him. Unsure whether or not to acknowledge him as he is wearing a German officer's uniform, Caldicott decides against the idea. He is sure that he knows him but equally he knows of no one in the German military; perhaps if he can get a better look at the man's face, he might be able to confirm who he thinks it is. Unfortunately, the Officer turns his back and Caldicott can no longer see his face. Perhaps he is mistaken; nothing is said and he follows Charters to leave the compartment. At the same time as they try to leave, an elderly gentleman tries to enter the compartment which causes some confusion in the tight space..

Charters, arrives at the door first, and says "Excuse me"; the elderly man politely steps aside to let Charters and Caldicott leave, just as they have been ordered to.

It doesn't take too long before Charters and Caldicott find another compartment, although not quite as empty as their previous one. Although they have to sit between other passengers they manage to find two seats opposite each other. Sitting there, Charters puffs on his pipe and Caldicott, having thought the matter through a little more, leans forward and asks "Did you notice that German officer, who came into our apartment?"
"Yes. Why?" replies his friend.
"Well I could have sworn that it was old Dicky Randall" continues Caldicott. "Dicky Randall?" enquires Charters.
"Yes we were at Balliol together. You must have heard me talking about him? He used to bowl slow leg breaks. He played for the Gentlemen once. Caught and bowled for the Junior Common Room"

Whilst they talk about Caldicott's time at Balliol, one of Oxford's oldest colleges, the train jolts into action and slowly starts leaving the platform and Prague behind them.
"Oh yes. Dicky Randall" says Charters, "but if he is a German Officer, how can he be Dicky Randall?" Charters.
"Well I know him quite well. His rooms were next to mine" explains Caldicott. "Why on earth!" says Charters before realising the implications of what Caldicott has just said, "You don't think he's working for the Nazis, like that fellow, what's' his name?"
"Traitor? Hardly old man, he played for the Gentlemen" says Caldicott confident in his knowledge of his old college friend's loyalty and patriotism.
Giving the matter a quick thought, particularly regarding his cricketing experience, Charters points out, "Only once!"

Nothing further is said and the train picks up speed as it leaves Prague Station behind and continues on its long journey to Munich. Charters settles down to read his copy of Mein Kampf whilst Caldicott smokes his pipe thinking about the slow leg breaks bowled by his old friend from Balliol and trying to provide a logical reason for the similarity between him and the German officer.

During the night, the train pulls up at a station; Charters and Caldicott look through the window to read the name, but it's not a stop that they recognise the name of. A whistle blows and the woman Station Master shouts "Everybody out at once please". Charters and Caldicott, along with all the other passengers, struggle with their luggage whilst wondering what on earth the problem might be. With their previous experience of trains and travelling through Europe, they consider either to be a faulty train or down to the usual burdens of bureaucracy. On their last journey through Europe, they had to spend the night in a village hotel in Bandrika due to a snow avalanche; being September, they know that it can't possibly be due to snow this time.

There are no porters and what makes it worse for the two English travellers, is that there is no platform where their carriage door is. Clearly the train has made an unscheduled stop at a station not suitable for the train. Off the train, Charters and Caldicott see the German Officer who Caldicott thought he recognised as Dicky Randall, his old friend from Balliol. Caldicott decides that it would be rude not to acknowledge his old friend and walks over to where he is standing in order to greet him; Charters follows him.
As they approach the German Officer, Caldicott asks "Oh I beg your pardon. Aren't you Dicky Randall?"
The officer replies "Major Herzoff, Corps of Engineers".
The two Englishmen are taken aback, this is not what they were expecting to hear; how could Caldicott be so mistaken?. Feeling embarrassed and quite foolish, Caldicott says "Oh, I'm frightfully sorry. It was very silly of me but it is an amazing likeness".
Charters, also disappointed, turns to his friend and adds "Never mind. Come along old man".

The station and the telephone

Charters and Caldicott leave the German officer and move further along the platform to try and look for somewhere to sit with their luggage. At the end of the platform they find a waiting room, where they enter and sit on one of the benches in the middle of the room. "You know you made me feel painfully embarrassed Caldicott" says Charters clearly disappointed in his friend and apparent inability to distinguish the difference between a German army officer and an old cricket playing college friend.

In his defence, Caldicott meekly replies "Well, I can't help it if old Dicky Randall has a double"

Charters continues with his rebuke, "Do you realise we are travelling in very difficult times" followed shortly after by a little snigger.

"What's' the matter?" asks Caldicott, confused by the snigger.

"I can't help thinking of your face when he said Major Herzoff, Corp of Engineers" laughs Charters.

Caldicott is not amused and retorts "All I can say Charters, is when it comes to humour we live in an entirely different world" They both sit in silence, Caldicott partly embarrassed about mistaking the German Officer for his old friend and partly annoyed with Charters for finding the situation amusing. Charters is equally embarrassed about the mistaken identity situation but his embarrassment is disappearing and being replaced by the humorous memory of Caldicott's face. He also feels a little sorry for his friend's discomfort.

The woman Station Master, who had so loudly asked them to leave the train without any explanation, appears in the waiting room. Although not far from where they are sitting, she shouts "Everybody to leave the waiting room". Seeing Charters and Caldicott sitting oblivious to her command she adds "unt you two please. Come on!"

Charters huffs "This is getting beyond a joke" Resolute in his determination that he will not move again, he defiantly sits back folding his arms.

Re-united in having a common foe, Caldicott joins his friend in defiance and adds "Yes we can't stand for this" and also sits back with his arms folded. Two soldiers, who have followed the Station Master in to the waiting room, see the downright refusal of the two men to follow the instructions to leave the waiting room. In order to support the command for everybody to leave the waiting room, they stride up to the seated Englishmen.

Charters nudges Caldicott who has not seen the arrival of the two soldiers. "No good being undignified old man" says Charters and stands to pick up his luggage. In his view, he has once more made a stand against bullying officialdom and once more retreated with his dignity still intact.

"Quiet right" agrees Caldicott, who likewise stands and picks up his luggage. They both leave the waiting room, dignified and heads held high, passing the two armed soldiers.

Charters and Caldicott are once more told to move

Ejected from the train, and also from the waiting room, Charters and
Caldicott make their way to the platform where they see a luggage
trolley standing on the platform. Empty of any luggage it looks like an
ideal spot for two weary travellers to sit and wait for their next train.
It's not quite as welcoming as a waiting room, but at least it provides
them with somewhere to sit, albeit without any dignity befitting the two
English gentlemen. Unfortunately for Charters and Caldicott, and
within seconds of sitting on the trolley their fortunes once again
change. The Station Master re-appears once more and once more
shouts out her officious instructions; she shrilly snaps at them "You
can't sit here"
"Why not?" demands Charters.
"This truck is required. Come on, off, off, off , off." she acidly replies.

Standing, Charters turns to the officious woman and drily says "Well
these bags are required too" pointing at his and Caldicott's cases.

68

Shaking her head at Charters, the Station Master waves her hand and continues to say "off, off, off, off" until Caldicott also stands.

Fully dejected and defeated once more by officialdom, the two English men pick up their cases. Completely irritated by their treatment throughout the journey, and wanting to show his annoyance to the woman standing in front of him, Charters turns to Caldicott and says in a loud clear voice "We have been pushed about from pillar to post by this railway ever since we got on the train".

Caldicott shows his understanding of the need to talk loudly and clearly when trying to make foreigners understand the English language and adopts the same approach as his friend. "Yes, everything we sit on seems to be required".

"Its' monstrous" adds Charters.

Looking at the Station Master, Caldicott says "We shall write to the company about this. You are not at war with England yet you know." Looking along the train, she replies, but with a hint of a smirk appearing on her face, "But you are mistaken. France declared war this afternoon unt England declared war this morning. So". She slaps her ledger book down on the trolley and with an air of superiority she defiantly pushes the trolley off along the platform. To Charters and Caldicott annoyance, they feel that she has once more won the battle, not just by reclaiming the luggage trolley from them but with way that she did it with her knowledge of Britain and Germany being at war, knowledge that they didn't have.

Charters and Caldicott watch the woman disappearing along the platform shocked at what they have just heard. They were aware of the problems facing Europe but never expected events to turn so serious that England would declare war on Germany; whatever happened to the 'Peace in Our Time' statement made by the British Prime Minister Neville Chamberlain? They sit on their cases quietly considering the serious nature of what has just been said. "War" says Caldicott. "Yes" sighs Charters as he drops his book on to the floor. All of a sudden a very serious thought enters his mind, "Good heavens!" he exclaims.

"What's the matter?" asks Caldicott.

Charters turns to look at his friend and replies "My golf clubs!"

"Where are they?" asks Caldicott.

"I lent them to Max in Berlin" says Charters, "Like a fool I said he needn't bring them back until next Wednesday." He stands, looks intently at Caldicott and forlornly adds "Probably seen the last of them"

Caldicott nods his agreement, "Yes, I expect they'll require them for something or other. I read in the paper that they are pulling up park railings". Unfortunately his words of wisdom are not helpful to Charters who retorts "Well, I don't see the connection old man".

"Well your clubs are made of steel aren't they?" asks Caldicott.

Charters realises the implications of Caldicott's question sighs "yes", nods his head and sits down forlornly.

"There you are then" says Caldicott triumphantly.

"With shafts too; especially made for me" sighs Charters as he stands forlornly next to Caldicott.

Caldicott realises that his explanation of what might happen to the steel clubs has added to his friends despair about not seeing his clubs for some time. "Why not get in touch with Max?" he says trying to be constructive.

"How?" asks Charters.

"On the telephone" replies Caldicott, "Ask him to send them to London immediately".

"Its' definitely a chance worth taking" agrees Charters eagerly nodding in approval, "I'll never be able to replace them". There may just be a chance, albeit very slight, of him being able to recover his clubs before they are melted down as part of the German war effort.

At that moment, a railway man, wheel tapper in his hand, approaches Charters and Caldicott and walks between them rudely brushing them out of the way. He bends down to inspect part of the engine's undercarriage. Confounded as he is, by this latest example of rudeness from the railway company, he ignores the man's impertinence; he has a more pressing priority. Sparked into action by his friend's suggestion, of telephoning to arrange the return of his beloved golf clubs, Charters goes to pick up his luggage. Caldicott follows suit, but realises that they have no idea where the public telephone is. Turning back to the railway man he asks loudly and clearly "ooh, err telephone?" as clearly as an Englishman can converse with foreigners!

The railwayman turns to face Caldicott and replies "Station Master's Office" and indicates with his hand a suggested route for him to follow.

70

Charters and Caldicott pick up their cases and make their way to the Station Masters office carefully following the directions provided. Entering the office, they see a German Gestapo Officer using the phone. He doesn't see them at first and carries on talking. Not deliberately listening in to the conversation, Charters and Caldicott overhear him say "Captain Schalker?, Karl Marsen here. I am speaking from Saale".

Before he says anymore, he notices Charters and Caldicott standing in the doorway and puts his arm out to prevent them entering any further into the room. It is apparent to Charters and Caldicott that he wants privacy whilst having the telephone conversation.

Charters acknowledges their intrusion into a private conversation and says "Oh, I beg your pardon".

He and Caldicott leave the Station Master's office and the door is smartly closed behind them.

Charters desperately wants to phone his friend, so he and Caldicott wait outside the Station Master's Office until the telephone becomes free. They presume that it is not unreasonable of them to expect the Officer to let them know when he has finished. They don't have to wait long before the office door opens and out strides the Gestapo Officer, although he neither acknowledges them nor does he say anything about the telephone now being available; he looks to be deep in thought. Charters taps Caldicott on the shoulder and indicates that perhaps they could now use the telephone in the office.

Inside the office, Charters picks up the telephone and automatically gets the operator. "Hello, I want a long distance call to Berlin, Oliver 2466" says Charters. Irritated by the questioning response from the operator, Charters snaps "Yes of course it is important".

Waiting patiently, Caldicott flicks through a pile of papers on the table next to the telephone; Charters glances at what his friend is looking at. "It's all in German" explains Caldicott seeing his friend's interest. "Humph" retorts Charters. Before he has time to add anything further, the operator comes back on the line. Caldicott only hears one side of the conversation but he is aware that Charters is not happy after hearing him snap "Well how long then?" immediately followed by "Oh all right!" as he slams the receiver down. He turns to Caldicott saying "The blasted junction is engaged by the military. They'll call me back"

71

With nothing to do but wait for the call back, they go to leave the office but not before Caldicott gets in another dig at the Germans "These people seem to have no idea of business as usual".

Outside the office, Charters impatiently paces up and down the platform; Caldicott follows him. Also pacing backwards and forwards is the Gestapo Officer; they pass each other without acknowledgement, each deep in their own thoughts. Whilst pacing, Charters and Caldicott observe the troops loading endless amounts of boxes and military equipment onto the train. They nod to each other knowingly about things to come; it is clear to them that Germany is stepping up its preparations for war against France and Britain. Before they have the opportunity to comment, they hear the telephone ringing in the office. "That'll be our call" says Charters and he and Caldicott both turn on their heels to head back towards the office. As they do, the Gestapo Officer also strides towards the office; it seems that he is also expecting a call. He gets to the office seconds before the two English gentlemen and slams the door behind him immediately shutting Charters and Caldicott out.
"I don't believe it" says Charters, "I bet it was my call".

Unable to access the office and telephone, Charters and Caldicott restart the task of pacing up and down the station platform. On their first leg of pacing, Caldicott notices something and points along the platform "I say Charters, there's another phone in there"
"Mmm, oh" replies Charters lost for words before finding a suitable reply "Lucky"
They immediately quicken their pace to the newly found office and telephone; Charters arriving first and picks up the receiver. "Hello" he says and again culminating in a shout "hello, HELLO". "Its gone dead" he says to Caldicott and then proceeds to click the receiver several timers in an attempt to bring it back to live and once more speaks into the receiver "hello".
"Why don't you try the thingamabob" says Caldicott. Charters looks him at quizally. "You know; the gadget" responds Caldicott nodding his head in an attempt to make himself understood.
Somehow, Charters understands what his friend is saying and tweaks a knob on top of the phone. He starts to say something, but is cut short to the extent that he steps back, puts his hand over the mouthpiece and says it's a German, nodding his head in the direction of the other office

"It's that chap out there". Caldicott looks in the direction his friend is indicating and through the glass window he sees the silhouette of the German Officer on the other telephone. He turns back to his friend and says "Well, perhaps he'll be off the line in a minute".

Charters is intently listening to the telephone conversation and shushes his friend to remain quiet.

"What's up?" asks Caldicott, interested to know what his friend is listening to.

"They're talking about what's his name, you know, Herzoff" replies Charters. Caldicott returns his gaze to the silhouette of the German Officer whilst his friend continues to listen in to the conversation.

Charters listens in to the conversation on the other extension.

The telephone conversation over; Charters and Caldicott watch through the window, as the Officer leaves the adjacent office. "What is it?" asks Caldicott.

Well as far as I can make out, Herzoff isn't Herzoff" says Charters finally replacing the receiver on its hook; he has a very worried look about him.

"What?" responds Caldicott.

"No, they are sending an escort to arrest him when we get to Munich"

"Yes" says Charters nodding in agreement and with a great deal of concern in his voice..

Just then they hear the Station Master's shrill voice again, this time she is loudly screeching "All passengers aboard" Whilst they hear her, they don't move, mesmerised as they are by what they have just overheard and deduced. That is, until they hear the whistle being blown and the strains of the engine as it starts to pull the long train away from the platform.

"Herzoff?" questions Caldicott.

Charters looks at Caldicott and replies "yes".

"Listen. If Herzoff isn't Herzoff", says Caldicott ignoring the interruption from Charters and continues with his explanation of what he understands "Well he must be Dicky Randall"

"Caldicott?" says Charters, alert to what is happening behind them "The train!" acknowledges his friend. They both realise that if they don't move fast then they will miss the train and their journey back home, never mind the implications of the overheard conversation about Caldicott's friend Dicky Randall.

Charters and Caldicott ponder on the meaning of what was overheard on the telephone.

A near thing

They both run as fast as their legs will carry them, picking up their bags and cases along the way, running along the platform to catch the train that is swiftly pulling away from them. Unfortunately they can't get to a carriage but they do just manage to pull themselves into a goods carriage with its doors wide open, near the rear of the train. As they pick themselves up off the floor of the carriage, they brush straw off their clothes "That was a near thing" says Caldicott, relieved at what they have just accomplished
"I thought we were going to be in this infernal country for the duration" replies Charters.

Oh my lord" exclaims Caldicott looking around the carriage. Charters follows his gaze and sees what is troubling his friend; a troop of German uniformed soldiers are all staring at them. The twenty strong troop of soldiers look formidable in their uniforms, particularly as Germany and England are now at war and particularly as the soldiers all have rifles. Charters and Caldicott glance at each other before quickly getting to their feet, not only to gain some respectability but also to gain some composure in front of their new foes.

"Not knowing quite what to do or say, they glance at each other again before once more looking at the soldiers, whose eyes are all staring at the two English men. Needing to do something quickly and without any fuss, Charters taps his friend on the shoulder and points to a door in the corner of the wagon. Stooping to pick up their travelling cases, they move quickly and silently to the door in the hope of leaving the wagon and soldiers behind them without further ado.

Approaching the door, one soldier partly blocks their way. Caldicott, as though he is a commanding officer inspecting his troops on the parade ground, firmly says to the soldier "Hold that straight old man" and moves the soldier's rifle into a more upright position, thereby enabling him and his friend to more easily pass.

As they leave the goods wagon and enter the next carriage, Caldicott closes the connecting door behind him. "What were you saying just now about something emerging very clearly?" says Charters.
Caldicott hesitatingly asks "I said?"
"mmm" encourages Charters.
"When?" says Caldicott.
"On the platform" says Charters.
"About something emerging?" queries Caldicott.
Charters nods his head in agreement.
"What what?" asks Caldicott.
The conversation is further confused as "Charters replies "What is what?". Caldicott is still no clearer and asks "What emerged? You never said"
"Oh" replies Charters.
Both Charters and Caldicott are confused by what each other has been attempting to say or ask, but equally they are both deep in thought whilst also look very disconcerted about what Charters overheard on the telephone.

"I'm certain Charters, that what I'm about to say is that we have stumbled upon something pretty serious" says Caldicott looking intently at his friend who is staring into the distance.
"No doubt which side that Randall is playing for" says Charters.
"Ours" replies Caldicott.
"Yes" his friend replies, nodding in agreement.

Charters and Caldicott meet a troop of the enemies' soldiers.

A sudden thought hits Caldicott, "Yes that is what was emerging so clearly" he exclaims, thinking about what his friend has just said.
Locking at his friend, Charters says "Well it's up to us to find some way of warning him".
"Come on, let's find him" agrees Caldicott leading the way along the carriage corridor. They pass through the carriages looking for their friend Dicky Randall.
As they pass two uniformed German soldiers deep in conversation, Charters says "Oh Caldicott?"
"Yes" says Caldicott.
"Do you think it wise bursting into this?" quietly asks Charters.
"How do you mean?" his friend replies.
Charters explains "Well I mean we've no proof that Randall is working for England"
"Well everything points to it" replies Caldicott.
"Yes, but is that enough. We're enemy aliens. These Nazis seem keen on their firing parties" suggests Charters

"Mmm" says Caldicott thinking aloud, "Oughtn't we let that stand in our way" stopping to turn and look at Charters.

Concerned at the way the conversation is heading and the way that his friend seems to be questioning his loyalty and patriotism, Charters stutters "Oh certainly not. I mean if we were certain. As it is we've got to bear it in mind".

"I don't see what else we can be doing" says Caldicott.

"For all we know, he may be an international crook" says Charters.

"Crooks don't usually play for the Gentlemen" insists Caldicott.

"Well Raffles did" retorts Charters.

Caldicott looks at the floor thinking what else he can say to convince his friend to overcome his doubts of doing something to help Dicky Randall. "That was fiction. Still you may be right Charters" and starts to walk further along the corridor.

He doesn't walk much further before Charters catches him up; they both decide to sit on their cases and think about the situation and what they could do and what may happen if they do something. Charters looks at a book he is carrying and turns to Caldicott "Still, if we were certain, we'd do our duty and take the risk"

"Yes, What!" replies Caldicott.

"As it is, I get on with Mein Kampf. I haven't got out of Hitler's boyhood yet" says Charters, looking at the book he has in his hand

Charters and Caldicott continue to sit on their cases in the carriage corridor reading, Charters reads more of Mein Kampf whilst Caldicott is busy reading the magazine he bought earlier that day. Moments later, a German Officer comes along the corridor towards them; nearing them he says loudly "Please" as he tries to pass them.

Charters response is "Oh sorry" but neither he nor Caldicott bother to stand to let the officer pass.

The officer tries to squeeze past the two sitting English men but deciding it inappropriate for a German Officer to be treated so disrespectfully, confronts them and demands "You don't choose to stand up when a German Officer passes?"

"We're English" replies Charters as a means of explanation.

The short but simple reply stuns the German Officer into momentarily silence; gaining composure, he says "Your Passports" and puts out his hand to demand that they hand them.

The two English men look at each other before silently agreeing to provide them; they retrieve the passports from their inside coat pockets. Caldicott hands his over first, followed shortly after by Charters.

"Oh, I beg your pardon. You are quite right, the English shouldn't stand up" the officer says with a smile and looking at the two men still sitting on their cases "They should go down on their fat bellies and crawl".

At this incredulous insult, both Charters and Caldicott stand to protest, "Now look here" demands Charters.

The German Officer smiles even more at his own cunning, "So you are standing up. Very well, we will generously permit you to run back to England. No doubt to find yourselves safe jobs". He promptly hands the passports back to the tricked and insulted Charters and Caldicott. "Meanwhile, you may sit down" finishes the German Officer walking along the corridor past them.

Charters and Caldicott watch him walk away from them, both seething with anger at the insult and wincing at the way that they were tricked into standing. "Fat bellies!" seethes Caldicott.

"Safe jobs!" retorts Charters.

"As if they weren't all taken by now anyway" adds Caldicott.

"Caldicott, this is absolutely and finally the last straw"

"Yes Charters" replies Caldicott.

"We'll warn Dicky Randall come what may" says Charters.

Both men are riled and want retaliation and revenge for all the delays, hassle and now insults from the Germans. "I'm with you old man. Its' things like that, that bring it home to you" says Caldicott

They both pick up their cases and walk down the corridor determined to take a stand against the tyranny and cunning of the German's.

Passing a compartment, they see Dicky Randall through the open door; a white coated waiter is taking orders for refreshments.

"He's in there" whispers Charters, "That Gestapo fellow is there too". Caldicott looks "Yes, a couple of storm troopers there"

"How the devil are we going to pass him the word without that fellow spotting us?" asks Charters.

"We've got to do it somehow" replies Caldicott. He stares at the compartment deep in thought, desperately trying to devise a plan whereby they can warn Dicky Randall.

79

"Of course he might come out for a minute, I mean most people do" suggests Charters hopefully.

"We must act Charters, its' no good hanging about on the off chance" insists Caldicott.

As they discuss what and how they can do something, the Train Steward closes the compartment door and walks along the corridor towards them "Excuse me" he says as he tries to pass them.

Charters and Caldicott stand to one side in order to let the waiter pass.

"Wait a minute" whispers Caldicott as an idea springs into his head, "that err, Steward".

"What about him?" asks Charters.

"Well, he's bound to come back some time and bring their order" says Caldicott

"By Jove, yes" replies Charters looking at Caldicott

Quick as a flash, Caldicott retrieves a piece of paper from his pocket and leans on the wall using it as a desk; he quickly writes a note on a small piece of paper. He writes;

> *If you are the Dicky Randall who played for "The Gentlemen", you are batting on a sticky wicket. If you want to know more, we are in the lavatory.*
> *Caldicott.*

Charters nods in approval at his friend's quick thinking.

It isn't long before the Steward returns; "Here he comes" whispers Charters who is keeping watch. He taps Caldicott on the shoulder, silently indicating the arrival of the Steward and to hurry with the note.

"Excuse me" says the Steward, trying to squeeze past Caldicott.

Charters turns round to face the Steward with the aim of giving his friend a few extra moments to finish writing the note.

"Oh what?, what time do we get to Munich?" asks Charters thinking quickly for a delaying tactic.

"In about thirty minutes sir" replies the Steward.

In the moment that the Steward is distracted, Caldicott lifts a bun from the tray and carefully places his folded note on the tray before covering it with the replaced bun.

If you want to know more, we are in the lavatory

The two Englishmen watch the Steward walks away down the corridor and Caldicott lets a smile cross his face as he replaces his pen into his jacket pocket.

"Alright?" asks Charters.

"Yes, I put it underneath the doughnut" replies Caldicott.

"Good" says Charters, before suddenly exclaiming "what?" as he gives his friend a concerted look. "Well, how do you know they are for him?"

"Well, I suddenly remembered that Dicky Randall always had doughnuts sent up to his room for afternoon tea" says Caldicott. Charters sees the brilliance of his friend's plan and chuckles; "Very clever of you old man"; pleased, he taps his friend on the arm in acknowledgement.

"We'd better get along there eh" says Caldicott.

"Right" replies his friend.

They walk along the corridor to collect their cases; Caldicott stops in his tracks as he suddenly realises something very important. With a fearful look on his face, he exclaims "Oh my lord!"

"What's up?" asks Charters.

"Well, I'm wondering whether it was doughnuts"

"What?" exclaims Charters.

"I believe it was rock cakes" says a worried Caldicott who continues with a meek "phew".

Looking at each other, they walk down the corridor towards the lavatory. Both apprehensive and worried, they realise that whatever happens now will happen, no matter what. There is no going back.

Although it seems like an eternity, they only have to wait a few minutes before the lavatory door opens and the German officer Herzoff, who they think is Dicky Randall, enters. He must have got the message and understood enough of it to meet the two Englishmen in this irregular manner. It is a bit of a squash with just two people in the lavatory, never mind three, the presence of another person makes it very cramped.

Major Herzoff, or rather Dicky Randall, starts the conversation, "Yes, I am Randall"

Caldicott takes his hand and shakes it keenly, "How are you old man; remember me?", glad that Major Herzoff isn't Major Herzoff but is his old school friend.

"Yes" replies Randall.

Caldicott indicates to Charters with a nod of his head "This is Charters, an old friend of mine".

Randall and Charters shake hands both saying "How do you do"

"Well what is it?" says Dicky Randall impatiently trying to get to the point.

Caldicott starts the explanation "Look here. We don't know what you are up to of course"

"Never mind about that" interrupts Randall curtly. He is annoyed with how Caldicott has put him in a potentially dangerous predicament and now insists on following protocols of polite chit-chat.

"But whatever it is" continues Caldicott, "you appear to be on the spot. Tell him about it Charters"

Charters picks up the story, "Well, I was phoning Berlin about my golf clubs. By the way I'm resigned to the fact that I shall never see them again for a while"

Dicky Randall is even more annoyed about this latest attempt at pleasantry when there are, in his opinion, more important issues to discuss. He impatiently snaps "Yes, but get on with it!"

Slightly annoyed about this disregard for his golf clubs, Charters says "I'm coming to it" and continues "I was telephoning on the other chap's line. You know, that Gestapo fellow. I overheard him saying that they were sending a military escort to arrest you when you get to Munich".

"You see, you're rumbled" explains Caldicott. "They know that you're not Herzoff".

Dicky Randall is not too pleased at this news, but nor is he rattled. He looks at the two Englishmen with great thought; "Now listen. I can't tell you everything, there isn't time, but I've got to get that old man and girl out of this country at all costs"

"What, an official job?" asks Caldicott

Dicky Randall nods and asks "Are you two fellows willing to help me?"

Caldicott asks "Against Germany?" to which Randall nods affirmatively.

"I say we are, after all they've done to us. What do you say Caldicott?" says Charters.

"Absolutely old man; backs against the wall" says Caldicott in agreement. "Mmm I hope not" adds a worried sounding Randall; the words 'backs against the wall' sounds too much like standing in front of a firing line; the usual end for a spy if caught in enemy territory.

At that moment, the train lurches and the three Englishmen are bounced around the cramped lavatory to the extent that Dicky Randall has to put his arm out to steady Charters against the lurching movement. "Steady" he says, "We need a little more room don't you think?" He puts his hand to his chin as he thinks out his plan, deciding what their next move should be to prevent the German high command from getting their hands on the old man and his daughter.

Dicky Randall (Rex Harrison) in disguise as Major Herzoff questions Charters and Caldicott on what they know.

Charters and Caldicott silently look on, pleased that they are doing something against Germany, even though they don't know who the old

83

man and girl are nor what their importance is, nor even what Dicky Randall's involvement in all this is. They wait for their instructions on how they can help Randall in his daring mission to get the old man and girl out of the country.

It isn't long before their plans and instructions are agreed and Randall leaves the lavatory; Charters and Caldicott are left with instructions on what they are to do.

Reiner and Reinemann

The exact details of the first part of the plan remain a blur but it's fair to say that Charters and Caldicott execute them swiftly and successfully. The two Englishmen, whilst matched in numbers, overpower the two German guards with the advantage of surprise. The two guards had been standing in the corridor and had not realised that Charters and Caldicott posed a threat to them until it was too late. Charters and Caldicott quickly change in to the uniforms removed from their captives, in order to disguise themselves. Dressed as German soldiers, the two English men are ready for the next part of the plan. They respond to the order from the Gestapo officer as he shouts the names of the two guards.

"Reiner! Reinemann!" shouts the Officer.

Approaching the Officer, Charters and Caldicott in disguise, see that it is the Gestapo Officer Marsen that they had overheard on the telephone. They also see that Marsen is holding a pistol pointed at their friend Dicky Randall. Worried that their rescue plan is falling apart, they see the need to do something, and to do it quickly before they are recognised. Their actions come as a natural instinct to them; they attack the Gestapo Officer. Assisted by Randall, who lashes out with his feet, they overpower him and manage to quickly disarm him. Marsen, the Gestapo Officer, had very nearly implemented his plan to arrest Randall and hand him over to the armed guard and to hand the scientist Bomasch and his daughter over to the German high command in Munich. With not much time remaining, it being only a few minutes before the train arrives alongside the platform in Munich station, there is just enough time for Dicky Randall to swap his German Officer uniform with that of his Gestapo foe, Karl Marsen.

There is just enough time for Dicky Randall to introduce Charters and Caldicott to the old man and the girl. They find out that the old man is Alex Bomasch and his daughter Anna. They also learn that Bomasch is a scientist that the Germans want to help in their war against Britain and realise the significance of the help that they have provided so far.

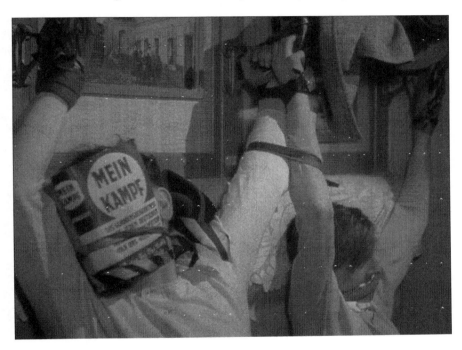

Captain Marsen (Paul Henreid) and his guard are left trussed up as part of the escape plan.

In Munich Railway Station, the train comes to a halt, Randall, dressed in Marsen's Gestapo uniform, takes Anna Bomasch by the arm and quickly leads her off the train, followed closely by her father. Charters and Caldicott, also looking the part in their German uniforms borrowed from the now unconscious Reiner and Reinemann, follow. Unsure as to exactly how to behave as German soldiers, they follow at a distance that they consider appropriate to their role as military guards. Dicky Randall stops the party on the platform in order to carefully assess the situation, and also to give his group a chance to get into their allotted positions. Randall only needs a moment and sets off with his two "prisoners", Axel Bomasch and his daughter. Charters, seeing the need to also move of, nudges Caldicott with his elbow and they follow, doing their best to imitate the appearance and behaviour of how they think German soldiers would behave in a real situation.

Charters and Caldicott in disguise as Reiner and Reinemann

A short distance along the platform, the group meet another group of genuine German soldiers marching towards them from the opposite direction. This is a critical point in the escape plan and any mistakes at this stage may be disastrous for the group of escapees. Randall stops his group in order to address the approaching German officer, saluting him with a Heil Hitler. The German officer returns the salute.
"I am under instructions from the Army Headquarters to arrest Major Herzoff" says the German officer.
"I hear he is a traitor" says Randall, "The prisoner tried to escape and I had to deal with him. You will find him in the last compartment of Coach 66".
The German officer acknowledges what he has just heard with a simple nod of his head and starts to go along the platform to find the carriage.

Before he gets far, Randall asks him "What, What transport have you?" "Excellent " he replies.

Randall continues with his deception and introduces the old man and his daughter. "This is Herr Bomasch and his daughter. To which the officer salutes in acknowledgement.

Randall continues "They are in protective custody and I have instructions to take them to General Von Manstein without delay. With your permission I will use one of the cars".

"Certainly" replies the German officer, unwittingly accepting the ploy. "I will leave you to take charge of the prisoner" says Randall. "Will you show me my car?"

The German officer instructs one of his guards by saying "Take this SS officer to the car" "Truck 66 you said?"

"The last compartment" answers Randall.

Charters and Caldicott feel slightly relieved that they've got this with the rest of their group. They move off, led by the German soldier allotted to take them, to where the car and driver are waiting. At the car, the German soldier says to the driver "Ottem, you will take the SS Officer and his party in your car" He stands to one side to let the party climb into the car.

Quick thinking, Randall says "One moment, can your driver be trusted?"

"Well, I think so" replies the soldier, "he is an old member of the party"

"A man to be trusted perhaps" queries Randall, "I think I would rather take one of my own men. I am travelling to the base with the greatest secrecy"

"Very good" replies the soldier obediently and turns to the driver and says to him "You will not be needed Ottem".

The driver, also a dutiful and obedient German soldier, acknowledges the order, "Very good Sir"

Randall turns to Charters and Caldicott with the order "Reimer, you will drive"

Not knowing which one of them is supposed to be Reimer, the two look at each other with trepidation. Not knowing what to do next is no good if the escape plan is to work. In order to moves things on quickly, and without raising any further suspicion, Randall salutes the guard, "Heil Hitler" he says.

Randall gets into the back of the car but Charters and Caldicott remain uncertain which one of them is supposed to be Remeir. If they had been quick witted, or at least had some thought about them, they would realise that it makes not bit of difference, as the guard knows neither of them. Nevertheless, in an attempt to continue with the deception they simultaneously salute the guard and say "Heil Hitler". This causes some bemusement with the guard but fortunately for the escapees, it does not raise any suspicion and the guard turns and walks away without saying another word.

Charters and Caldicott in disguise as German soldiers in the getaway car

Relieved, Charters and Caldicott get in to the car and close the door. "Come on quick" says Randall realising the urgency to get away from the station as quickly as they can; after all any more cock-ups and they may be rumbled.

The Swiss border

Charters drives the German military car at a steady pace so as not to draw any unwanted attention to the fleeing group. "Right man, right. You're not in England" shouts Dicky Randall just as the driver of an oncoming car hoots his horn at them as a warning to get out of his way.

"Oh, I'd forgotten" says Charters almost apologetically, steering the car towards the right hand side of the road; if only foreigners drove on the proper side of the road like the British do, he thinks.

Munich and the railway station and any immediate danger are a long way behind them; it is night time and the group travel fast through open countryside. The group are more relaxed since the start of their escape at the station, confident in thought that their escape plan might actually work.

Caldicott is no exception to this growing confidence of the group and he lets his mind wander to life back in England including cricket amongst other things. He turns to his friend driving the car and says "I was just thinking Charters; in the last war, the army took over Lord's cricket ground for growing food on"

Charters replies "I wonder if they'll do it this time?"

"Short sided you know" adds Caldicott.

Charters is lost for words at the thought of this possible desecration of his beloved Lords cricket ground and nods in agreement.

Randall leans forward, not to join in the discussion of war and the conflicts it may have with cricket, but to give further instructions. "You'd better pull up here Charters" he says, "We can't get through to Switzerland by the main road; let me take over will you?" Charters nods in agreement and slows the car down.

Several miles later, with Randall driving, the landscape of the German countryside changes from flat farmland, to rolling hills to alpine mountains with hair pin bends, steep inclines and sharp drops at the side of the road. Dicky Randall continues to drive as fast as he can, keen to complete the escape into Switzerland.

Caldicott turns to him and says "There is one thing that is worrying me Randall old man. It may be silly of me of course, but exactly how are we going to get across the Swiss frontier?"

Without taking his eyes of the road, Randall coolly replies "I know a place where I used to go climbing at about eight thousand feet up, where Germany and Switzerland meet"
"You're not going to ask us to hang about on ropes I hope!" asks Caldicott
"I'm not" replies Randall. "But they may. There's a narrow road that leads right to the top".
"What's over the top?" asks Caldicott.
"Switzerland" came the cool reply.
"Anything between?" continues Caldicott
"A six thousand foot drop" replies Randall drily, still driving the car as fast as he dare

Caldicott is nervous at this last bit of information; he needs to know more about how they will continue with their escape into Switzerland "Well …. How can we?" he asks.
Randall interrupts him "Skip it"
"Skip it?" asks Caldicott wondering why Randall doesn't want to discuss it.
Before Randall can continue with his brief and concise escape plan, Anna Bomasch, sitting in the back of the car with her father sees something behind them in the distance, shouts "There's a car following us"
"Is there?" asks Randall, looking through his rear view mirror. "Well here we go" He changes gear, puts his foot down and turns right off the road onto a narrow and steep lane just narrowly missing a horse and cart that is just turning into the lane from the opposite direction. The road climbs higher and higher into the snow covered mountains, but Randall doesn't slow, he is doing his damned best to get Bomasch and his daughter to safety.

They don't travel too far along the lane before the car reaches a teleferic station at the border between Germany and Switzerland. They all quickly clamber out of the car and rush to the building; Randall is the first to get there.
Just before he opens the door, he turns and shouts "Watch the road, Charters".
As he enters the building Randall shouts loudly "Anybody here?" He is closely followed by the others.

90

Caldicott the last to enter the building, asks "Anybody around?" Nobody answers.

They make their way across the station building to where they can see the cables leave to stretch across the valley disappearing into the distance. Randall points out across the valley and says to Caldicott "Switzerland there!"

The group turn as they hear somebody enter the room and say "Good morning to you sir, good morning". It is an old man, presumably the teleferic operator in charge of the border crossing. He walks across the room towards the group busily fastening his jacket as though he has just been disturbed from his rest.

"Are you in charge here?" asks Randall.

"Yes, there is only me" replies the old man.

"I want to cross to Switzerland" states Randall.

"Now sir?" asks the old man quizzing.

Randall replies "Yes", firmly

"But there is a war" states the old man, "I had orders yesterday to close the telecage"

Randall stands to attention and curtly says "My orders come from the highest source" Dressed in the Gestapo uniform and barking orders should be enough to satisfy the old man's inquisitiveness, but he persists with his questions.

"Higher than the Chief of Police at Matzburg?" questions the old man.

"Gestapo headquarters at Munich" replies Randall.

"Oh" the old man is convinced by Randall's lie but nevertheless unclear how to respond to the conflicting orders.

Randall follows up with his act and says "I have orders to escort this lady and gentleman safely out of Germany".

The old man realises he has no alternative but to follow these new set of orders and says "I had better ring Christopher"

Before Randall has a chance to find out who Christopher is, Charters turns from the window from where he has been watching the road. He has seen something and needs to tell the others. "A car is coming, it looks like them"

Momentarily stunned into silence, the group stand looking at each other. "Keep an eye on them" says Randall; Charters rushes back to take his position at the window.

At the border

Meanwhile, the others turn and watch the old man who is still on the telephone; hopefully Christopher is his counterpart at the other end of the cable car in Switzerland. They overhear him say "Yes thank you Christopher. I've got it and the butter"

Perplexed but mostly concerned about the crisis unfolding before him and the lack of urgency on the old man's part, Randall snaps "Do you want me to report you for incompetence?" The old man quickly realises the implications for his own safety if he continues chatting with his friend, so takes a more official approach and continues "They'll be leaving in about two minutes Christopher". Putting the phone receiver down, the old man turns and walks towards the group "I shall require to see your papers. Have you got any passports?"

Randall ignores the question and instead asks "How long does it take to cross the valley?"

"About four minutes" replies the old man.

"Once its' in mid air, can it be stopped?" asks Randall

"Why yes sir" replies the old man, "If anyone wanted to stop it. Will you follow me to the office".

The old man leads the way to the office, "This way please"; Randall follows, not to produce papers, which he does not have, but to do something about the old man. As the teleferic operator enters the office, Randall leaps into action, pulling the door shut and locks the old man inside the office. He has managed to put him out of action without injuring him.

"Can you see them?" asks Randall as he rushes over to where Charters is stood.

"No, but I can hear the engine" he replies.

Randall turns to see Caldicott studying the cable car controls and says "How does this thing work?" Caldicott doesn't know but he continues to look at them intently trying to figure out how they work.

However, the old man Bomasch, after quickly looking at them, seems to be able to work the controls and says "That shouldn't be difficult".

"But how" demands Randall as he removes his overcoat.

"Obviously this starts it" says Bomasch, pointing to a lever.

"Yes" replies Randall clearly encouraged by the scientist's knowledge of machinery, but still wanting to know more, and quickly too.

Bomasch continues looking at the other controls and indicates the next one that he understands, "The speed regulator"

"The speed regulator" repeats Randall in acknowledgement

"Right; quick. Get in, all of you" shouts Randall, "Quick, Caldicott" and pushes his fellow escapees into the cable car.

"What about you?" asks Anna Bomasch of Randall, realising that Randall intends to stay behind to operate the controls to enable them to escape.

"I'll start it and then jump on" says Randall unconvincingly.

Charters is still at the window and seeing the car carrying the German soldiers approach the teleferic station, he turns and shouts "They are here". He quickly leaves his post at the window, as Randall shouts to him "Come on, jump in"

"They'll stop us half way" says Charters realising the desperateness of the situation.

"Get in will you" snaps Randall as he stops the car for Charters to get in. Charters jumps in and Anna Bomasch says to Randall "Come on, quickly"

Randall knows that he needs to stay behind to ensure that the others escape across the border into Switzerland. There is no alternative if he is to succeed in doing his duty; he has no option but to ignore her. He restarts the cable car.

The car starts moving again and the group look on hopelessly as they see the German soldiers trying to get into the building where Randall stands guard over the controls. It isn't long before the soldiers realise that their quarry is escaping and start firing on the cable car, either in the hope that they will maim the rescuers or to kill Bomasch; either way they need to prevent the scientist from escaping. One of the shots finds its target and smashes the glass window of the car; fortunately it fails to hit any of the occupants.

Stating the obvious, Caldicott says "They've shot at us. Get down" and he proceeds to shut the adjoining open window as though that will provide some protection from the rifle shots. Crouching down out of sight, the group are covered with pieces of glass as a second shot smashes through the window shattering the glass to smithereens; so much for closing the window thinks Caldicott.

Three more shots hit the teleferic, but thankfully none of the escaping passengers are hit. Caldicott, having initially forgotten that he has a rifle as part of his disguise as a German soldier, suddenly stands to use it. He uses the butt to knock the remaining glass out of the smashed window and starts to return shots at the German soldiers. Charters follows suit and they both start firing at the German soldiers who are firing at them from their position on the mountain side next to the teleferic station.

Out of rifle range, the teleferic car slowly but surely approaches the Swiss border; Charters, Caldicott, the scientist Bomasch and his daughter Anna watch through the window, the unfolding events back on the German mountainside. It doesn't take long before they reach the Swiss station where they quickly leave the teleferic car. Safely in Switzerland and out of harm's way, they are desperate for some sign that Randall will also be able to reach safety. Several shots ring out across the valley before they see the teleferic car next to them jolt into movement. Realising that Randall is working the controls to get it moving again and also that the one on the German mountainside opposite them will also be moving, they allow themselves some hope that he too will make it to safety in Switzerland. Watching with bated breath, they see Randall on the German mountainside jump into the moving teleferic car just as a small group of German soldiers appear in the station building. The soldiers shoot at the teleferic car carrying Randall and Randall returns shots. The Germans know that Randall is fast moving out of range of their rifles; they also realise that they can shorten the range by reversing the car's destination. The group in Switzerland see the two teleferic cars stop in mid flight and then reverse direction, so that the one carrying Randall is returning to Germany.

Again, shots fire out at each other from the Germans and Randall. Charters and Caldicott continue watching, helpless and not able to provide any assistance to Randall. One by one, shot by shot, Randall gets the German soldiers in his sights and slowly reduces their number until only the officer remains. Ever closer to the German border, the cable car returns to its original position, with Randall trapped aboard it; returning him to certain death at the hands of his nemesis, Marsen the Gestapo officer..

Charters and Caldicott fire at the Germans trying to break in to the Teleferic station.

Charters and Caldicott realise the dire consequences that awaits Randall if he is captured alive; as a British Officer disguised as a German he will be tried as a spy, with death in front of a firing line being the only outcome. They gasp with renewed hope when they see Randall hit the remaining German soldier. Wounded, the soldier stumbles to the ground, but with sufficient strength to finish his duty, the soldier watches as the cable car carrying Randall continues to bring his prey nearer to capture and ultimately to be shot. Nearing mid point between the two cable car stations, the escapees on the Swiss side of the border see how desperate the situation is for Randall; there is no escape for him. Or is there?

Randall climbs onto the roof of the teleferic car; unsure of what he is about to do, all that Charters and Caldicott can do, is watch. He steadies himself as the two cars approach each other ready to pass in mid-air and it becomes apparent to the observers, exactly what he is planning to attempt. Hundreds of feet in the air, dangling between the two mountain borders, Randall leaps from one car to the other and somehow manages to take hold sufficiently to clamber aboard the car bringing him to Switzerland and safety.

The two English men stand side by side with Alex Bomasch, the professor and his daughter. The group show their happiness and emotion in two very different styles. Bomasch and his daughter Anna, shout, laugh, weep and hug each other. Charters and Caldicott in true English style, smile, nod to each other and shake hands as if to say 'a job well done old man'. They are proud to be British and proud to have thwarted the German enemy.
They watch, smiles on their faces, as Randall approaches the Swiss border unhindered, his safety assured.
The only remaining thing for Charters and Caldicott to do is to work out the next leg of their journey back to England; travelling across Germany by train is certainly not an option now.

Crook's Tour

Crossing the desert

Charters and Caldicott are sitting, or rather sleeping, on a tour bus operated by Spindles Tours. The bus bounces along a very poor dirt track that in the desert is called a road. Charters and Caldicott are bouncing backwards and forwards; after a hearty lunch, this and the heat of the sun, has the effect rocks them in and out of sleep; they have both fallen deeper into sleep, from which they are not immediately woken when the bus comes to a crunching halt. Unbeknown to the two sleeping English travellers, the tour guide explains in faltering English that the bus has broken down and tells the other travellers that they need to get off the bus.

Moments later, Charters stirs from his slumber, awakened by the bustle of his fellow passengers leaving. Seeing the exodus, he gives Caldicott a sharp nudge with his elbow.

"Hey, hey, Caldicott, Caldicott" he says trying to stir his friend. Caldicott, sleeping with his hat pulled right down over his head as a means of securing some shade in the hot desert, stirs.

In response to the nudge that awakens from his deep slumber, and accompanied with a large yawn, he says "Yes; are we there?"

A fellow traveller exiting the open windowed bus, hears Caldicott's question and replies "Lord no, the bus has run out of juice"

"But that's absurd Charters, what a pest" says Caldicott. Charters smiles but Caldicott is not best pleased; he turns to the tour guide and angrily snaps "You told us that this trip was only going to take a day". The man replies "Oh I say, I say, old chap. I can't be blamed". Caldicott realises that he should not have blamed the man like that and half apologetically says "It will probably cause a rift between Edith and myself that's all. She'll be waiting in Budapest thinking that I'll be on my way and I'll be sitting on my err .., in a charabanc. Its err, fantastic" "My dear fellow" replies the man in consolation.

Charters continues to describe the poor situation that they find themselves in by saying "All night in the desert, no bed, no bath". He waves his right arm annoyingly towards the desert, before continuing with his woe is us speech, "Sleeping with people who we have never been introduced to. It places us in a very very disagreeable position". He shuffles uneasily in his seat.

The trip across the desert was only going to take a day.

Caldicott whilst listening to his friend, surveys the desert surrounding the tour bus and sees movement in the distance beyond the monacled Englishman. "Look, what's all this?", Charters turns to look where his friend is indicating, as do the two remaining passengers.
"It's the first thing we've seen since we left Baghdad" says Caldicott as they all go to leave the bus by climbing down the steps at the back.
In the distance, they see a group of riders dressed in the native Arab clothes; not exactly a usual sight in these parts of the world, but nevertheless quite strange to Charters and Caldicott, particularly when they see that the riders in single file are not on horseback but are riding camels.
Intrigued by what they see, Charters and Caldicott think it a jolly good idea to get a closer look at the camel riding group and head off towards the riders who are still some distance away. Caldicott takes the

100

opportunity to use his binoculars and study the group in more detail.
"I think they are coming this way" he says to his friend.
"A fine looking lot" replies Charters.
Caldicott passes him the binoculars and says "I once read a book about a girl who fell in love with a shake"
"Sheik is the correct pronunciation" corrects Charters
"Both Sheik and Shake are Arabic" suggests Caldicott
"A comic son is hardly a criteria whilst smiling in a condescending manner" says Charters sarcastically.

Charters watches the approaching Arabs through his binoculars and exclaims "ooh, ooh, I say a nice bit of horse he's got there. Good Lord!. He's making straight for us" with some concern, he turns and faces an equally concerned looking Caldicott.
"Do you know any Arabic, Charters?" asks Caldicott
"No, I do not" replies Charters with a degree of trepidation, "It's going to be a bit awkward"

The Arabic horse rider approaches the two English men and Charters greets him by raising his pith helmet and loudly says "Good afternoon" He continues talking loudly and slowly "My name is Charters" Not knowing what else to say to make himself understood he replaces his hat and nods vigorously. "You wish, to me, to speak" he continues. Clearly understanding Charters, the Arab replies "Yes, I am the Sheik Abdul Ramda". Surprised that the Arab can speak English, Charters turns to look at his friend a few feet behind him. Sheik Abdul continues "I came over to see if I could be of any help, but". He momentarily stops speaking as he sees something familiar about Charters and points. "I know that tie! You see, I too went to Marlbury"
Charters smiles and replies "Well, well. You are an old Marlburian?" As the sheik replies "Yes", the two shake hands and they all chuckle. Sheik Abdul explains "I left there in nineteen hundred and eight".
"Oh, that will be a little before your time" he adds noting that Charters looks younger than he.
Charters nods his head and chuckles ""Yes, I was 1912" and turns to Caldicott to say "Oh, what a funny thing" He turns back to the Sheik and apologising, points to Caldicott. "This is Caldicott, my friend"
The sheik mutters "Not a Marlburian?"

101

"Rather" says Charters with a hint of embarrassment, "yes he was at Granton"

"Oh really!" says the Sheik "We had the annual cricket fixture with Granton"

Charters chuckles again and replies "I kept wicket for the first eleven"

Charters and the Sheik both chuckle again.

"He was the Granton team's lead bowler"

Familiarities over, the Sheik looks at the two English men and asks ""What are you doing here? Has your bus broken down or something?"

"Yes" replies Caldicott "It looks as though we are going to be here for the night", Charters nods in agreement.

"Oh oh, that's awkward. I ought to be able to help" says the Sheik. "Look here, I'm pitching camp close by for the night. Would you like to join me for dinner?"

"I would be charmed, yes" says a grateful Charters and turns to Caldicott saying "What about you Caldicott?".

"I would be delighted" says an equally please Caldicott..

"Very well" says the Sheik, "Shall we say 9 O'clock in my tent?"

Charters and Caldicott reply almost in unison "Oh thank you, very kind of you"

"Now I had better see if I can arrange accommodation for the rest of your party" says the Sheik. "But for the moment, Ma'a salama" and gestures with his hand to head and mouth, before riding off. The two Englishmen say "Goodbye" as Charters waves.

"Charming fellow, isn't he?" says a smiling Charters.

He turns to look at a disconcerted Caldicott who replies "I say Charters".

"What?" he asks.

"This presents a bit of a problem" says Caldicott.

"What do you mean?" asks Charters.

"We haven't got dinner jackets" explains Caldicott

"Good lord, no" says Charters twigging on to the predicament that the two English men now face. His face lights up and says "Oh, well after all we would look rather silly, shouldn't we? Sitting on cushions in a tent in the middle of a desert"

"Well the natives might expect it" suggests Caldicott.

Later that evening, Charters and Caldicott are sitting on stools next to a short table with Sheik Abdul in his tent. Given his importance in his home country, the sheik is accompanied by a tall guard who stands, discreetly, a short distance behind him. The three men are singing the old school song from Marlbury which Charters and the Sheik both attended. As they sing, two maids arrive; one removes a plate of left overs whilst the other places a large bowl of fruit on the table. The singing stops and Charters taps on the table in a jovial attempt to get his friends' attention and says to Caldicott, "Oh no, you've got it all wrong old man"

Slightly dismayed at the comment, Caldicott replies "Well no, not at all. You were out of tune"

"Well surely, Ramla and I know the Marlbury song better than you" states Charters.

Ramla, the Sheik laughs and diplomatically intervenes, "Well, perhaps if my musicians were to accompany us, Mr Caldicott will find it easier, eh?" he says.

"What" exclaims Charters sitting upright, "Do they know it?" and points at the musicians

Ramla replies "But of course, I taught it to them myself". He claps his hands for the band to start playing. The three sit and watch the band play the Marlbury song using musical instruments, that whilst unfamiliar to the two Englishmen, they presume to be Arabic. The band start singing the words to the song, that they have been meticulously taught; a big smile beams across Charters' face and he looks proudly across to Ramla. For a short while he attempts to conduct the musicians using his arms in the manner that a conductor would use his baton. "What memories this brings back" he proudly says.

His new friend, Ramla the Sheik, agrees and says "I shall never forget the year the day that we beat Harrow"

"Ooh, Ooh" agrees Charters "Close finish, wasn't it?"

Before Ramla can reply, a serving maid arrives with glasses of water and smiles at Caldicott; he returns her friendliness with an even bigger smile.

The thought of cricket prompts Charters to say "Ooh I say Caldicott, talking of Lords. We shan't be in time". The smile quickly disappears off Caldicott's face and he looks worryingly across at Charters.

"Are you returning to England?" Ramla asks as he pours brandy for his guests.

"Yes, we promised ourselves to see the last test match" replies Charters.

"As a matter of fact" adds Caldicott, "this breakdown has messed up our arrangements. I was going to meet my fiancé"

The maid returns in to the tent with candles and cigarettes. Charters watches with a slight concern as he sees his friend smiling whilst watching, or rather admiring, the maid. Feeling the need to cut in and divert his friend's attention and with a hint of disapproval in his voice, he says "Yes, he was meeting his fiancée, my sister you know. Caldicott is engaged to her"

"Oh really" says Ramla as the maid lights Caldicott's cigarette.

Caldicott, still smiling, is oblivious to what is being said and can't take his eyes off the maid. That is, until he sees Charters scowling at him.

"I must congratulate you Caldicott" says Ramla.

"Oh thanks" says Caldicott "Yes, heaven knows when I shall see her again now"

"I think I can get you back to Baghdad by tomorrow evening" assures Ramla which makes the two English men look at him with amazement.

"You can?" asks Charters

"Can you really Ramla?", adds Caldicott.

"Of course" assures Ramla rolling his glass between his hands and smiling at the two English men. "I hadn't realised that you are in such a hurry. I'll lend you two of my fastest camels"

"Camels?" says Caldicott, looking very concerned.

An equally worried looking Charters stutters "You mean!" and then feebly attempts to recover his composure by saying "Oh I see"

Ramla asks "You are quite used to camels, of course Charters?"

"Oh yes, yes, rather" he replies unconvincingly, before turning to ask his friend, "What, what do you say Caldicott?"

Caldicott also doesn't want to lose face and therefore without any real alternative he reluctantly agrees "mm, fine, marvellous"

Before they can be questioned further on their camel riding abilities, the maid returns and curtsies to the Sheik and discreetly relays a message to him.

"Will you excuse me for a minute" Ramla says to the two Englishmen, rising to act on the message.

Charters politely agrees "Oh certainly" , but only just before Ramla rushes out of the tent.

Charters and Caldicott, both still sitting, lean towards each other over the table. Caldicott carefully looks around the tent to check if anyone is around that could overhear them. "I say, I can't think why you said that you'd ridden a camel before?" he says.

"Because it's true, I have ridden a camel" retorts Charters

"When?" asks his friend.

"When I was a little boy" came the reply

"Where?" asks Caldicott

"The zoo" explains Charters

"Hardly any experience of much benefit now" sneers Caldicott, unhappily.

Caldicott asks Charters about his camel riding ability.

Their friend, the Sheik, returns and says "I'm so sorry. We have to be on alert and ready to deal with any emergency these days"

"Yes, I suppose these tribal fellows are a pretty wild lot" agrees Charters with a smile. The Sheik looks at the two smiling innocent Englishmen, who are seemingly pleased with their assessment of the difficulties facing the Sheik. The Sheik returns their smile and says to clarify, "No, no, your real Arab is all kindness and has real loyalty to your country. But there is some foreign power working in their ranks trying to make trouble, particularly in the oil fields"

"Oil fields eh?" enquires Caldicott.

"Yes" says Ramla "Guarding the pipeline is our great difficulty. Until we can find out who is responsible for the unrest, things won't be easy. But I shouldn't be worrying you with all this. I have arranged beds for you and one of my men will wake you in the morning".

They all stand to leave and Caldicott says to the smiling Sheik "Well, thanks very much". Charters adds his gratitude by adding "Yes, that's very good of you. I hope that we're not putting you to too much inconvenience"

"Oh no, not in the least" says Ramla, "If one old Marleyburian can't help another old Marleyburian"

"Hurrah" says a smug Charters "Yes, I see what you mean. Marleybury forever, eh Caldicott?"

"Absolutely, old boy" readily agrees Caldicott and picks his glass and proposes a toast. Both Charters and Ramla follow Caldicott's example. "As an old Grantonian, I salute you Marleyberries". All three raise their glasses to the toast and drink.

The following morning, the two Englishmen are standing next to a camel. Caldicott is hot and bothered and has his helmet shoved to the back of his head. Being an English gentleman, he still wears his jacket and tie, even in these very hot climates. The similarly attired Charters mops his brow with a handkerchief, as the camel standing next to him seemingly stares with a hint of disdain.

"Don't take any notice old boy" reassures Caldicott seeing how the camel looks at his friend.

"How do they expect us to get right up there" says Charters gesticulating with his hand to the top of the camel's hump.

"Oh, I don't know" replies Caldicott "I hope that we're not making ourselves look very ridiculous; especially in front of the Berber" indicating the man holding the camel by its stirrups.

"Here, here, give me a hand" says Charters walking around Caldicott to the front of the camel. Taking hold of the saddle he jumps up, whilst simultaneously pulling on the saddle, trying to mount the animal. Caldicott tries to assist by firmly pushing his friend upwards. The first attempt is unsuccessful, but the two persevere and try again.

Unbeknown to Charters and Caldicott, their antics have drawn a crowd of amused Berbers, who watch the hilarious antics with a great deal of amusement.

Charters tries a different tactic to mount the camel, by raising his leg so that he can put a foot in a stirrup in the same way that he would mount a horse. Again, Caldicott assists by pushing his friend from the rear. The camel, being much higher than a horse, remains unmounted as this new tactic also fails to work..

For all the pushing, pulling and stretching by Charters assisted by Caldicott, the effort gets them nowhere and the two Englishmen momentarily give up. Charters turns away from the camel and scratches his head in the remote hope that a new idea will come to mind. "Oh this is impossible" he eventually says, "you know Caldicott, I can't help thinking that if we had one camel with two humps instead of two with one, it would be a lot easier"

Standing back to reassess the tactics that have so far failed, Caldicott concentrates on straightening his hat which was partly squashed by Charters during his attempts to mount the camel. After a moment of serious thinking, he says "Well the whole trouble is that the thing is too steep of course"

Not really listening to Caldicott, Charters continues "If it was a two humper we could fit between the humps" and uses his hands to illustrate his explanation. Caldicott is reasonably happy with his now straightened hat and puts it on his head. Looking at Charters he asks "Well, how would there be room for both of us then?"

"Well" Charters replies "I don't know. If not, one of us could sit on a hump and the other sit in between".

Caldicott isn't convinced and studies the camel for further inspiration. Continuing with his solution, Charters adds "and every so often, we could stop the camel and change places" Caldicott starts to see some sense in what his friend is proposing but asks "Oh, How do you?"

"What?" asks Charters

"Stop the camel" continues Caldicott.

"Oh I don't know" retorts Charters "I suppose they stop of their own accord"

"Supposing they don't" queries Caldicott

"In that case, you tire the bugger out" adds his friend.

Not convinced, Caldicott says "You'll look rather ridiculous to go cantering into Baghdad and out of the other end"

Charters is indignant with his friend's unnecessary humour and says "Well guess what, lets concentrate on getting to Baghdad. We'll never catch that connection".

Before the discussion gets any hotter, they are interrupted by the Sheikh saying "You just go".

Charters and Caldicott are embarrassed; they politely chuckle to each other. Not knowing exactly what to say Charters starts to say something but the only words that come out are "Oh, well, Err, yes, we will be, as soon as we get on"

The amused Sheikh says "Ah, do say if you'd rather go by the coach. It is all ready. We managed to get it fixed up for you".

A relieved Caldicott says "ooh, that's fine" and smiles at an equally smiling and happier looking Charters.

Charters claps his hands and adds "that's absolutely marvellous my dear fellow. Oh yes, oh rather". He looks at Caldicott before saying to the Sheikh "Caldicott wasn't very keen on the camel"

Displeased with the way his friend has cast him, Caldicott says "Don't be ridiculous"

"Well, you'd better hurry, the others are waiting" says the Sheikh

"Oh that's a pity" says Caldicott trying to bluster away his embarrassment about not being able to mount the camel "I was getting quite fond of that camel" Just as he says this, the camel turns his head to look at the two Englishmen as if understanding what has just been said and gives a knowing look.

The dance of the veils.

The two travellers continue their journey across the desert through Saudi Arabia and Iraq by coach without any further incidents. They also make their connecting train to reach their next destination of Baghdad. Disembarking from the train at Baghdad Station, Caldicott waits in the central station concourse whilst Charters goes to enquire at the ticket office about the next leg of their train journey.

Charters arrives back with the news "The next train leaves at five to twelve so we've got an hour left to kill"

"Well I could do with a bite" comments Caldicott. Charters agrees "mm, I'm a bit hungry too" . "Where shall we go?" asks Caldicott. They both look around to find somewhere close by where they can eat.

"What about that?" says Charters seeing somewhere that may be of interest and grabs his friends arm to show him where he is looking. Charters has seen an advertising board which says

Baghdad
Folies de Londres
Avec
Les Girls
LA PALERMO
Dans
LA DANSE D'HIBOU
(La Danse de Vailes)

"Mmm" they both say as they try to read the sign. "It looks a bit continental doesn't it" says Charters. "I expect its one of those places where there's lots of dancing girls"
"Oooh, do you think so" says Caldicott, more than slightly interested at the sound of dancing girls.
"Oh yes" replies Charters, "Look what it says, La Palermo in the dance of the owl, the only owl dance in the world" clearly confident in his understanding of French.
"Owl dancing?" queries Caldicott
"Mmm, I believe there used to be a girl who did a dance with a swan. I suspect that it's much the same thing, except with an owl" answers Charters.
"Curious" Caldicott says, "I don't suppose that there will be much on anywhere else"
"There's not much on here either" says Charters "Come on let's go and check"

The two English men arrive at the club and looking around the foyer, Charters says "A bit Raffish isn't it"
"Oriental architecture you know" replies Caldicott knowingly.
They both approach the cloakroom desk and simultaneously say
"Good evening" to the attendant in response to his greeting of "Good evening gentlemen"
"You can leave you're your hats" he says.
"Thank you" replies Charters taking a ticket from the attendant and passes his hat to him, but not before giving Caldicott a knowing look. Caldicott repeats the action and also says "Thank you".

The cloakroom attendant points the way saying "Straight down the steps gentlemen".

Charters and Caldicott walk in the direction that has been pointed to them. "I don't suppose we'll see those hats again" sneers Charters. "You're developing a very suspicious mind" replies his friend.

"Hey do you think it's alright?" asks Charters, worried at the sort of establishment that they have entered. They stand at the entrance to the ballroom area, watching several scantily clad girls dancing on the dance floor. "It looks pretty good to me" reassures Caldicott, pleased that there are dancing girls, as promised by the poster at the railway station. A small orchestra plays at the back of the dance floor beyond the dancing girls, which adds to the atmosphere, the presence of the orchestra, in Charters view, gives some respectability to the place. Charters and Caldicott decide to stay and have a drink; descending the stairs, the Maitre'd greets them "Good evening gentlemen"

"Good evening" replies Caldicott.

The Maitre'd asks "You desire a table?"

"Yes for two please" replies Caldicott.

"Certainly sir, this way if you please" the Maitre'd says and leads the way around the edge of the dance floor. As they follow, Charters and Caldicott watch the dancing girls; Caldicott like what he sees, but not so Charters. Caldicott is mesmerised, after all, you don't get this sort of performance back in England. His friend does not like what he sees and worried about the sort of establishment that they are in.

They are shown to a table, quite close but not next, to the dance floor. Seated, they both light cigarettes. Wanting to see more of the dancing girls, but not quite wanting to admit to it, Caldicott asks "Are you sure you wouldn't like to be nearer?"

"Positive!" his friend disdainfully replies looking closely at Caldicott and adds "I don't want to appear Victorian but is that the sort of display that you'd like to bring Edith too?"

"But we haven't brought Edith!" Caldicott replies.

"True Caldicott" Charters says before sarcastically adding "but you are engaged to her"

Dismayed by his friend's uncalled for assertion, he replies "And what is more Charters, it never occurred to me to bring Edith to a show like this"

"You don't understand" his friend reassuringly says "I was only pointing out…"
Before he can explain further the Maitre'd returns with the menus. As they take one each, Caldicott says "Oh thank you" to the Maitre'd. Charters tries to read the menu but Caldicott doesn't bother; his eyes are concentrated on the troupe of dancing girls.

Charters reads the first page of the menu,

Soup or Hors d'Euvres
Fried Fish
Potato Hot Pot
Or
Seikh Kebab and Rice
Or
Wine Leaves Dalma
Bucklava or Kounafa
Coffee

Caldicott takes a turn at looking at the menu and drily says "Well speaking for myself, I prefer something that they can't half mistake in Arabic"
"In that case, what about the soup?" suggests Charters
"Good idea, order it" agrees Caldicott.
Looking at the waiter, Charters says "Potage celery please waiter".
Caldicott looks at the waiter too and adds "Same here please".
"Ah yes sir' and to follow?" the waiter asks.
Caldicott studies the menu before saying "Oh here's something that I had last time I was in New York. A sort of fried chicken!"

Charters agrees to his friend's suggested choice, "By all means" and leaves Caldicott to attempt to order in his best French, "poullez Maryland please"
The waiter, slightly confused by Caldicott's attempts at French, thinks he understands him and says "Poullez Maryland?" for clarification.
"Yes that's alright isn't it?" asks Charters.
"Oh yes sir" says the waiter, "anything else?"
"Have you a wine list" asks Charters
"Yes sir, here it is" and passes it to Charters who says "Oh thank you".
Caldicott is largely oblivious to his friend's conversation with the

waiter, due to the fact he is unable to take his eyes off the dancing girls. However, he notices that Charters has asked for the wine list and says ""I'll leave the choice of wine to you Charters. I think that's more up your street"

"Up my vineyard" chuckles Charters clearly amused with his little joke.

The head waiter (Morris Harvey) waits for Charters and Caldicott to decide what to eat.

Caldicott smiles, not at his friend's joke, but at the girls on the dance floor. He also doesn't hear what Charters next says; "Ooh I say, here's a bit of luck. Here's one I can vouch for", for he is too busy grinning widely at one of the girls who is sitting rather provocatively on the dance floor near to the English men. As she sways her arms to the rhythm of the music, Caldicott's smile grows wider and wider.

Oblivious to where his friend's attention is directed, Charters continues discussing the wine that he has some knowledge of, "I drank a bottle only last summer with old Fruity Watkinson. Yes you remember old fruity." Looking at Caldicott, he stops mid sentence; he sees where

112

Caldicott is looking, and who he is grinning at. He is dismayed at what he sees. The girl that Caldicott is grinning at is sitting nearby on the dance floor now with her legs tucked up behind her raised arms.
"Caldicott!" he snaps.
Caldicott quickly averts his gaze and momentarily loses his smile before gaining a sheepish replacement. H looks at his friend who says with a hint of exasperation, "I do wish you would pay attention. If you could tear your eyes away for just one moment".
In his defence, Caldicott says "What just occurred to me" and points to the dance floor "that it is supposed to represent a harem"
"I was about to order wine" retorts Charters who stabs the wine menu angrily with his finger.

"Oh splendid" says Caldicott, "Go ahead"
"Alright then, a bottle of fourteen" says Charters, "la fit Bothschild 1929" to the waiter. Charters wonders why the waiter looks back at him in such a peculiar manner. "What's the matter?" asks Charters
"Oh nothing sir" and repeats the order "la fit Bothschild 1929?"
"Yes, well that's what I said" says Charters perplexed.
"A very excellent wine sir" replies the waiter before walking off.
Charters and Caldicott watch as he walks away. Charters leans across to his friend and says "I could have sworn that that waiter just gave me a wink"
"Probably something in his eye" suggests Caldicott, "The place is full of untidy eaters" and he looks around the room as though to confirm his suspicions.

It isn't long before their soup arrives and Charters is the first to start; Caldicott is too busy watching and clapping the dancers as they come towards the end of their routine. "Well that's that" says Caldicott and picks up his spoon to take his first taste of the soup.
"Good, now you'll be able to get on with your soup" says Charters sarcastically.
"I was merely allowing it time to cool off" explains Caldicott, annoyed at the implication behind his friend's comment.

La Palermo (Greta Gynt dances the Dance of Veils

As he finishes speaking his eyes are drawn to the dance floor again by the sound of clapping in response to another dancer arriving on the dance floor accompanied by what looks like an owl.
"This is the turn we saw advertised old boy" says Caldicott rather excitedly.
"So I gathered" disdainfully replies Charters, looking up to see what all the fuss is about.

On the dance floor, the young woman starts singing

> "There's no need for lovely phrases of sweet delight.
> There's no need of speeches coming from you
> All the words are there, revealed in those big brown eyes
> Giving away your thoughts, telling me all.
> You don't have to tell me.
> Its' written in your eyes"

Caldicott is mesmerised and is lost in the words and beauty of the woman and her singing.

"Every time you look at me
Something seems to tell me
You are all so very wise
Every time you look at me
Seems love and cooing
Would appeal to you
Now I think that you would like to"

At this point the well trained owl, emits a too whit too woo in time with the music. Caldicott is impressed.

"You don't have to tell me
Its' written in your eyes
Every time you look at me"

As the music continues, the singer glides across the dance floor, occasionally kicking her legs up and twirls around. She does this right in front of Charters and Caldicott;. Charters is neither impressed nor amused by a scantily clad woman gyrating and cavorting in front of his very eyes; he looks at her with disdain. Caldicott sees her very differently from his friend and says "I say, she's a stunning looker old boy" as he takes a piece of bread from his plate.
"Hardly my type" sneers Charters, "Comparatively well-dressed by local standards though" almost as a half-hearted compliment trying not to be impolite.

The singer continues gliding and swirling across the dance floor; at the next table that she stops in front off, she seductively removes one of her veils and throws it to one of the diners.
"Did you notice that" says an amazed Caldicott to a now smiling Charters, "she accidentally dropped one of her veils". Charters stops smiling at his friend's innocence and replies "I don't think it was an accident old man"
"What?" says a still smiling Caldicott
The dancer drops another veil before making her way across the dance floor back to near where Charters and Caldicott are sitting and throws a veil onto Caldicott. Grinning like a Cheshire cat, Caldicott pulls the piece of silky material off his head and looks across at Charters.

Charters is not happy at his friend's behaviour; not only does he consider that he is inappropriately encouraging the girl, he also thinks that his sister's fiancée should not be behaving in such a manner. As the young woman dances away from the two Englishmen, she throws her last veil to another group of diners revealing what she is wearing, or rather not wearing beneath her costume of veils. The remaining costume consists of very little, apart from a jewelled and sequined tiny top and bottoms set. The audience clap very excitedly, as does Caldicott.

The mood of the entertainment subdues as the singer leaves the dance floor and some sense of normality resumes to Caldicott. Charters and Caldicott wait for their food to arrive. Whilst waiting, they enjoy a glass of white wine and watch as a young woman approaches them; "Good evening gentlemen" she says, "would you like to buy a record" and offers them a 78rpm record in a white card sleeve from the top of the pile of records she is carrying.
"Well no thanks, we are just going" says Charters.
Presuming that the record is of the singer he has just enjoyed listening to and watching, Caldicott asks "Well how much are they?" as he nonchalantly flicks the ash from his cigarette.
"250" replies the woman.
Charters looks at his friend and with a hint of disdain says "You don't want one of those things old man". Ignoring his friend's advice, Caldicott gets his money from his trouser pocket and carefully counts out the notes.
The woman sees him looking at his friend and considering his advice, so she steps up her sales pitch by saying "I think you do sir"
"Well I certainly don't" says Charters and continues to drink his wine. After counting out the 250, Caldicott returns the rest of his money to his trouser pocket and says "Well. I'd like to have one as a souvenir"
"Thank you sir" says the woman and places the record on the table and takes the money offered by Caldicott before moving to the next table. Proud of his new purchase, Caldicott studies it with some pleasure; Charters looks at him with a hint of disdain. "Remind you of the glad eye she gave you. I suppose" he says.
"I think that is very uncalled for" replies Caldicott, "As a matter of fact, I thought that it might appeal to Edith".
Charters picks up his drink and looks at his friend; before he takes a sip he says "I can't imagine anything less likely to appeal to Edith"

Rebuked, Caldicott sits silently reading the notes written on the record sleeve.

Charters drains his glass before replacing it on the table and looks at his friend. Almost instantly regretting the harsh words used, he taps Caldicott on the sleeve and says "Oh come on old boy, come on drink up. We'll miss the train"

He sees the waiter not far away and raises his arm to catch his attention and indicate that he wants to settle the bill.

Having paid the bill, Charters and Caldicott leave the dining room and make their way over to the cloakroom to collect their hats. Although there are two gentlemen already standing at the counter, Charters goes straight to the front of the queue to hand over his ticket, saying "Two hats and a taxi". The two gentlemen look at Charters, annoyed at his impudence in taking their rightful place at being served first.

"Taxi in five minutes sir" replies the cloakroom attendant.

"Don't you realise that we have got to catch the train for Istanbul" snaps Charters. At this juncture, one of the men stood at the counter turns to face Charters and demands "Hey, what is all this?" His American accent gives away his nationality

"I phone for taxi" explains the attendant.

The man's colleague argues with the attendant "You get our checks, we're in a hurry" whilst still glaring at Charters.

"So are we" replies Charters, "We've got a train to catch"

"Ah, nuts!" the American exclaims, waving his hand at Charters and his impudence. He turns to his friend and says "Come on". They both walk away in disgust and head towards the dining room. As they leave, Charters and Caldicott over hear him say "These guys are screwy".

"Americans, I presume?" says Charters knowingly.

Istanbul

Sometime later, Charters and Caldicott having taken the train to continue their journey to Istanbul in Turkey via Mosul in Syria, are standing outside Istanbul Station. Holding their suitcases, the two English men momentarily pause to take in the views. "Well, here we are old man, Istanbul, the gateway to the East" says Charters. Although the sun is shining and the temperatures are hot, the two Englishmen are typically dressed for a British summer, wearing suits and carrying overcoats. Charters wears a chequered dicky bow whilst his friend sports a stripy tie. Looking around, they see a man, a short distance away, watching them. Suspicious, Charters turns to his friend and says "On your guard old man, one of those Spindles guides has his eyes on us" The man is dressed exactly how one would expect a tour guide to dress, wearing a light coloured jacket with black trousers and shoes and white shirt and tie. On his head he is wearing a black and white peaked hat. "Keep him off, or we'll be on another charabanc tour" adds Charters.

Caldicott nods in agreement and says "Too late, he's bearing down on us".

The tour guide purposefully walks over towards Charters and Caldicott and politely but informally salutes in the way that somebody touting for business would. "Good morning gentlemen. Are you travelling with Spindles Tours?" he asks.

"No, we are not" snaps Charters

"We've had quite enough of Spindles" adds Caldicott

"Yes, one of your charabancs broke down in the desert and we were in it" explains Charters.

"Oh dear" says the tour guide, "It is my duty to make up for this unfortunate accident"

"I'm afraid" Caldicott starts to say.

Before he can continue, he is interrupted by the tour guide saying "If you are looking for a first class hotel, undoubtedly the best in Istanbul is the Hotel Hamilton"

"Look, my friend has just told you" says Caldicott to the smiling tour guide.

The tour guide interrupts him again by adding "The rooms are most comfortable gentlemen" As Charters rolls his eyes, the tour guide continues explaining the merits of the hotel by saying "and the cooking is excellent" and puts his hands to his mouth to emphasise the excellence of the food.

Despite his initial reservations, Charters is interested in this last description of the hotel's merits and asks "The cooking is good eh?"

The tour guide, with growing confidence that he has secured his customer, adds "The Hamilton has the best restaurant "

"What do you think Caldicott?" asks Charters

"I'll leave it entirely to you" replies his friend.

"Well it's only for one night" says Charters, "the Budapest plane leaves in the morning"

"Alright then" agrees Caldicott

The tour guide pleased with his impending commission smiles and says "The hotel is this way sir"; taking Charters' case, he leads the way to the hotel. Caldicott carries his own case.

The hotel is only a short walk from the station and it only takes a few minutes of following the tour guide before Charters and Caldicott find themselves in the foyer of the Hotel Hamilton. As they cross the foyer, the concierge sweeps his arm and greets them "The Reception is on the left gentlemen" he says.

The two Englishmen follow his directions and cross to the reception desk where two receptionists are stood. "Good afternoon" says the receptionist with a smile.

Charters and Caldicott simultaneously return the greeting "Good afternoon". Charters adds "We want two single rooms for the one night. How much is that please?"

"With bathrooms sir?" asks the receptionist

"Well naturally!" replies Charters

"350 piastres each" says the receptionist

Having booked in to the hotel, Charters and Caldicott set to leave the reception area, the receptionist says "I'll telephone the chambermaid to draw your baths right away"

Caldicott smiles and says to his friend "Very inviting girl that"

"Mmmm, trifle anxious about having to bath ourselves though" replies Charters.

"Natural enough" responds Caldicott as he looks around, "probably a feature about the place".

Slightly concerned about what he thinks his friend is hinting at, Charters expresses his concern with a "mmm". They follow the porter carrying Charters' case; he is tasked with showing them to their rooms. Once again, Caldicott is left to carry his own case. Before they start ascending the stairs, the two Englishmen stop to have another look around the reception area. From this vantage point, they can see into the bar area where they see, and also hear, a woman singing.

"I say," says Caldicott, "See who that is"

"Yes, yes it's La Palermo" says Charters nodding his head.

At the thought of La Palermo, Caldicott smiles dreamily with fond memories of their previous encounter. Charters seeming to know what he is thinking, scowls at him. They both walk over to the bar lounge and stop at the doorway where they can better watch La Palermo performing on a small stage at the far end of the room. She is accompanied by a trio of musicians, one playing the cello and two violinists. As the two English men watch her singing, La Palermo recognises them and gives them a big smile. Caldicott smiles back, and carries on smiling, until Charters notices what he is doing and catches his eye with a big scowl. Ignoring the fact that his fiancées' brother is annoyed with him, Caldicott turns and once more dreamily smiles at the sight of La Palermo.

She sings the line "One night of heaven with you" and Caldicott turns to his friend and says "A very attractive girl you know".

Still not entirely happy with his friend's unseemly behaviour, Charters retorts "Try to remember that you are still engaged to Edith".
"Yes, I suppose I ought to send Edith a telegram saying that we won't be there until tomorrow" says Caldicott, thinking of Edith but not really acknowledging his friend's concern.
Being reminded that his sister will be on her own in a strange city for the night, Charters exclaims "Ooh good lord yes yes", straightens his bow tie and continues "Well, you'll probably be able to send one from here. Go and ask over there" and indicates the reception.

Caldicott walks over to the reception where a dark haired receptionist has now replaced the blonde one and asks "Can I send a telegram from here please?" She replies "Well yes sir, of course. I take it down for you" and she picks up a pencil and a pad of paper.
"Thank you" says Caldicott and proceeds to dictate the telegram.

They eventually make their way upstairs; Caldicott is still carrying his case along with his overcoat and hat, whilst the porter carries Charters'. As they reach their rooms, the porter lets them into the first room followed by the two Englishmen. "All looks very nice" says Charters. "Not bad at all" agrees his friend, before adding "What about meeting in half an hour's time in the lounge?"
"Why don't you have first bath?" suggests Charters
Caldicott politely declines "No, no you have first".
"Oh it's alright, I can wait" says Charters
"Alright, no point arguing about it" his friend politely agrees.

Caldicott sees the porter waiting in the doorway in order to show him to his room, so he leaves the room to find his own.

Caldicott is pleased to see La Palermo again, but Charters is not so sure.

On his own, Charters glances around the room and just as his eyes rest on the dressing table, the telephone rings. Perplexed and wondering who can be telephoning him, Charters answers the phone "Hello, yes" The woman's voice on the other end of the line replies "Are you listening?"

"Hello, who is it?" enquires Charters

The caller doesn't say who it is but mysteriously says "Get out of the hotel at once, and your friend. Do you hear me? Get out." The female caller raises her voice and adds "If you stay"; she suddenly stops mid-sentence and the line goes dead.

"Hello, hello" shouts Charters through the telephone receiver and clicks the phone cradle several times to try and reconnect to the mysterious caller; all to no avail. Looking at the handset he exclaims "Extraordinary thing" before replacing it. He repeats aloud to himself what he has just heard "Get out of the hotel, that's absurd. We've only just come in"

Wanting to know what Caldicott thinks to the strange conversation, he strides out of the room and walks along the corridor to the bathroom that guests have to share. Before he gets there, he sees what he thinks is Caldicott leaning over the threshold to the bathroom as though he is looking for something dropped on the floor. He approaches him and says "I say Caldicott" and taps him on the shoulder. The tap on the shoulder clearly startles him into losing his balance and falls forwards. As he falls, he lets out a very loud scream. To add to Charters amazement, the falling man doesn't hit the floor, he continues falling through a large hole in the floor.

"Good lord" exclaims the shocked Charters, who looks through the hole to see where his friend has fallen. He can't see his friend, but what he does see shocks him even more. At the bottom of the hole is what appears to be a fast moving river.

"Caldicott, Caldicott" he shouts to no avail.

"Caldicott! How deep is it?" he shouts again "Hold on Caldicott, I'm going to dive in. Hold on Caldicott"

Charters is distraught with worry for his friend's life. Before he can do anything to help save his friend's live, Charters hears a familiar voice saying "Hold on to what old man?"

Strangely, the voice sounds more than familiar and somewhere behind him along the corridor; Charters stands to see who is talking to him.

He can't believe his eyes, there walking nonchalantly along the corridor with his hands in his pocket is Caldicott.

Charters is shocked and almost lost for words, Caldicott, Caldicott" he stutters. "Its' you"

"Of course it's me" replies his friend "Always has been as far as I know"

Still shocked, Charters asks "But, are you alright?" and places his hands onto Caldicott's chest and feels to see if he is real and not some ghostly spirit.

Puzzled by his friend's strange behaviour, Caldicott replies "Yes. What's happened? You look as white as a sheet".

"But, but, but it wasn't you?" stutters a credulous Charters.

"Who?" asks his friend.

"Well you" exclaims Charters, "You were standing in the doorway and I, I slapped you on the back"

"I beg your pardon" asks Caldicott even more puzzled than before.

"Well, it wasn't you then" asks the Charters still stuttering.

Caldicott is confused but more concerned about by his friend's seemingly poor state of mind and once again asks "Who?"

"Well the chap I tapped on the back. He fell in"

"Where" asks Caldicott.

For the first time since the incident, Charters starts coming to his senses and realising that whoever the chap was that he tapped on the back and who consequently fell in to the hole to his certain death, clearly wasn't his friend. He realises what has happened. He needs to think clearly and quickly and quietly says to Caldicott "Sssh" "In here" he adds and indicates the bathroom behind him, Before they enter the bathroom, they both pause in the doorway and closely inspect the floor, or rather what is left of the floor.

"My goodness" exclaims Caldicott, "There's no floor".

"That's what I mean" says Charters "Its' a trick of some sort"

"Just a sheer drop" adds Caldicott

They both carefully step away from the doorway before Caldicott asks "What's down there?"

"Water" replies Charters and says "ssh, can't you hear it. It's the Bosphorus"

"Well that's very dangerous" says Caldicott "I might have stepped in and". The thought of what could have happened him stops him mid-sentence.

"I know" interjects Charters, "Its' labelled Bathroom"

"Well that's ridiculous" says Caldicott, "It should be labelled Bosphorus"

Charters and Caldicott return to the safety of Charters' hotel room where they try to phone the reception desk to explain, or rather to try to work out, exactly what has happened. Unfortunately, no one is answering.

"Can't you get them?" asks Caldicott.

"No; no reply" replies Charters. "Oooh that reminds me" he continues, "The most extraordinary thing"

"Eh?" queries Caldicott who is busy pacing up and down the bedroom.

"Yes. That's why I was looking for you. Somebody rang me up" explains Charters.

"Rang you up?" asks Caldicott. Charters replies with a non committal "mmm".

"Who?" asks Caldicott, struggling to try and make sense of what his friend has just said.

"Well it was a woman" says Charters. "An English woman; she told me to get out of the hotel"

"Why?" asks Caldicott.

"I, I, I don't know says a stuttering Charters. ""The line went dead"

Intrigued, Caldicott scratches his head and says "Well this is very extraordinary"

"Well that's what I thought" replies his friend.

"You know Charters, this is a very peculiar hotel" says Caldicott.

"Yes, and a very inefficient one too" agrees Charters.

"Well what about hopping out and going to another place?" asks Caldicott.

"I'm all for it" came the reply.

"Good. After all, there are limits" says Caldicott

"Mmm" agrees Charters

Caldicott returns to his room to collect his belongings while Charters also packs his luggage.

A short while later they meet up in the corridor. As they descend the stairs, Charters turns to his friend and asks "what about that fellow?"

"What, the man you pushed overboard" says Caldicott.

"The man I brushed against" snorts Charters, having regained his composure and feeling it necessary to defend himself.

"You'd better mention it on the way out" suggests Caldicott.

"We had!" retorts his friend.

As they reach the reception area, Caldicott glances around and seeing nobody says "The place seems to be empty"

Charters also looks around and is also amazed to see no one at all and confirms "There is no one at the desk".

"There doesn't seem to be a soul in the place" adds Caldicott. Unlike any other hotel they have stayed in, the whole place is strangely empty. There being no one to explain why they are leaving or what happened upstairs the two Englishmen quickly leave the hotel.

Outside on the street, Charters walks away from the hotel briskly in an attempt to leave the whole episode behind them. He turns and notices Caldicott behind him walking slowly. "Come along" he snaps, "Can't you walk a bit faster old man?" Caldicott doesn't hear his friend but is

124

looking around the place and says "There doesn't seem to be a taxi anywhere you know. I've been thinking about that extraordinary business of the man in the bathroom or Bosphorus room" and quickens his pace to catch his friend up.

"I can't make that out at all" adds Charters

"No. You don't think we ought to go and tell the police or something" asks Caldicott.

"A shocked Charters turns to his friend and says "Oh no, I might have to go and appear in court" before he continues briskly walking along the street.

"Hardly!" exclaims Caldicott.

"I might even be charged with murder" says Charters suddenly stopping dead in his tracks, contemplating the seriousness of his predicament and how the police might view the matter.

"Hmm" thinks Caldicott out loud.

"What?" asks his friend.

"Well it's impossible. I mean we've got a pact with Turkey" says Caldicott.

"That doesn't give me diplomatic immunity old man" snaps Charters, "Besides, think of Egypt and the Duke of Wellington's death. To say nothing of the West Indies Test Match"

"Oh no, we mustn't miss that" says Caldicott, clearly shocked at the thought of missing the test match. A test match that they have both been looking forward to attending at the end of this journey

Standing there looking for a taxi, Charters says "Well it's no use standing here talking. I don't like this place, let's get on to Budapest"

"But the train doesn't leave until tomorrow morning" points out Caldicott.

"We'll take a plane" suggest Charters, "There's a regular service I know. It says so in my guide book"

"Alright" agrees Caldicott, "anything to get out of this place"

"Here's a taxi" shouts Charters as he spots one approaching along the road

They flag the taxi down and as they climb in Charters says to the driver "The airport please".

A short taxi ride later, Charters and Caldicott find themselves in the airport departure area. Needing to confirm their travel arrangements, they approach a man in uniform. "When is the next flight to Budapest?" asks Charters.

"Oh very soon now sir" came the reply, "have you much luggage?" Caldicott replies "No, only these small cases"; turning to Charters, he says "Lucky we sent our other luggage onwards Charters"

The uniformed man says "Will you go over to the desk and take your tickets. There's just time to have your luggage examined" and indicates the ticket desk.

"Thank you" says Charters. He turns to Caldicott and says "The first bit of luck we've had so far". Relieved, they both walk over to the ticket desk.

It's the wrong room

Charters and Caldicott safely in Budapest, having found their hotel without any further mishaps, they enter the hotel reception with a little trepidation. The Hotel Manager approaches them, "Good evening" he says, "Welcome to Budapest"

"Good evening" the two English men reply in unison.

Charters asks "We err, want two single rooms"

"With bathrooms?" asks the manager.

Charters looks at Caldicott as he remembers his experience in Istanbul. "Have they got baths in them?" asks Caldicott with trepidation

"But of course" says the smiling manager, not quite understanding the question. "I will give you two splendid rooms with bathrooms. If you would care to register", he adds and indicates to the reception desk.

At the reception desk, the manager says "Rooms 47 and 48 sirs"

The two English men sign the hotel register and Charters turns to the hotel manager to say "My name is Charters; I believe my sister may have arrived"

"I do not recollect the name. One moment" replies the manager. He turns to the receptionist and asks her "Is there a Miss Charters staying in the hotel?"

"No sir" she replies.

Charters has already heard her reply, but nevertheless the manager repeats this to Charters "No sir".

Caldicott having completed registering his stay at the hotel joins Charters and the hotel manager and joins their conversation.

"Well after all, we did say tomorrow in the telegram didn't we?" says Caldicott.

"Mmmm, that's right old boy" agrees Charters, "Well I think I'm going straight off to bed".

"Suits me" agrees Caldicott.

"Will you be dining gentlemen?" asks the manager.

"No, no thanks. We'll go straight up to our rooms. I really must have some sleep" says Charters.

Caldicott adds "I feel as though I have been up for weeks". He picks up his case but doesn't notice that a bell boy picks up his friends case. The two of them follow the bell boy up to their rooms; Caldicott once more carries his own case without any offer of assistance.

The two travellers are both tired from the two days of travelling from North Africa and across Eastern Europe. Their shocking experience the previous night adds to their tiredness and they go straight to bed. Almost within minutes of their head hitting the pillows they are both fast asleep.

In his bedroom, Charters and weary from his travels is fast asleep, when suddenly he is awoken by the sound of ringing. It is his bedside telephone; he lets it ring a couple of times before answering with a very annoyed "hello"

On the other end of the line he hears his sister Edith. Without any hint of doubt he detects that she is annoyed with him, "No doubt you have forgotten my existence, but this is Edith" she says.

"Oh" Charters chuckles, oh hello Edie, old girl. So you've arrived uh?"

"I arrived in Budapest six hours ago." she retorts, "Since then I've been dragging my elf around all the hotels in the city enquiring for you and Sinclair. It is now ten o'clock at night and I find that you have quite typically retired to bed"

"Oh but", Charters asks, "didn't you get our telegram?"

"I received nothing!" says Edith indignantly; "When I got here I thought at least you would have sent a message to Spindle's office"

"But we sent the message from Istanbul" explained Charters.

Edith is even more annoyed; she is annoyed for not being able to contact her brother and now further annoyed with his continued insistence that he sent a telegram despite her repeated telling him that she had not received one. She is indignant at being contradicted and finally snaps, "Hawtrey, get out of bed. I must see you immediately"

127

Charters tries to reason with her "Edie, hang on a minute"; his attempts to placate her are to no avail as she has already hung up. Exasperated with her constant moods of indignation, Charters puzzles at what all the fuss is about on this occasion; he looks at the receiver before replacing it on its cradle.

Next door in room 48, Caldicott is also suddenly awakened, not by the telephone as Charters was, but by a large crashing sound from within his room. "What's that?" he loudly asks, reaching over to switch the bedside lamp on in order to better see. Sitting up, he looks around and is startled to see a young woman standing in his room looking at him, dazzled by the brightness from the bedside lamp cutting through the darkness. Looking closer, he recognises her as the singer from the hotel in Istanbul. "Good Lord!" he exclaims.
"Oh, I'm so sorry" says the startled woman, "It's the wrong room. I must have made a mistake"

Caldicott is not happy about the unwarranted intrusion in his bedroom and feels need to get out of bed to remonstrate with her. "Mistake! I like that" he shouts, striding across the bedroom to find out what the hell is going on. Seeing that she has his recently acquired record in her hand, he grabs her by the wrist. The young woman struggles to escape from his grip, but Caldicott continues to chide her by saying "You can't come charging in to a man's bedroom and steal his record"
Still struggling, she shouts "Let go"
Caldicott is not going to let her go without an explanation, but being a gentleman, he doesn't want to unnecessarily hurt or frighten her. Holding her wrist with both hands, he reassuringly says "I don't want to hurt you, but this is my room" This approach doesn't have the calming effect desired by Caldicott and the woman continues to struggle. She breaks free and shouts at him "If you don't let me go I will bite you"
"Unless I get a satisfactory explanation I shall telephone the manager" snaps Caldicott.
"And I've done nothing, I tell you" comes the response.

Not having received a satisfactory explanation, Caldicott attempts to recover his record that he considers that the woman has been trying to steal. "Well, what are you doing in my room?" he demands before lunging again in an attempt to recover his property.

Succeeding to get hold of the record, he wrestles it free from the woman's clutches. As he does, the bedroom door behind him opens; he turns to see who has come to his assistance. It is Charters and his sister Edith, the very same Edith that he is engaged to be married to. Standing there in the doorway, Charters scans the scene in front of him and is both astonished and shocked at what he sees, "Good heavens" he exclaims and walks across the room to where Caldicott is standing in his pyjamas next to the young woman. Edith follows.

"Oh hello Edith" says Caldicott with a little smile to greet her, "This is a surprise. I, err, didn't know you'd got here"

Angrily, Edith glares at him and snaps "Obviously"

Being an English gentleman, Caldicott considers it only proper that he introduces everybody to the woman in his room. He turns to the intruder and says "This is my fiancé and this is Charters". He then continues to introduce the woman, but not remembering her name he says "This is thingy me bob; she dances with an owl"

Charters is absolutely livid at this affront to his sister and snarls "Caldicott!, Really!"

Edith is very hurt but also angry and snaps "I think I know now why I never received that telegram"

Standing in his pyjamas in front of his exasperated friend and his fiancé who considers herself betrayed, Caldicott has no option but to try and explain what has happened. "Edith, you don't understand".

Before he gets any further with his attempts to clear his name, Edith interrupts "The situation speaks for itself"

Caldicott desperately tries to explain "But Edith, you must listen to me"

Charters also tries to bring some reasoning to the situation, "Its' not as bad as it looks Edith; it's probably only an infatuation"

"It's nothing of the sort" retorts Caldicott, "I was lying".

"I don't doubt it" interrupts Edith.

Caldicott continues and points to the bed, "I was lying there and she came in"

Charters, not wanting to hear any further says "Kindly spare my sister the sordid details"

"Quite" says the stony faced Edith and turning to her brother says "Perhaps you will take me to my room at once Hawtrey. I find the atmosphere in here very nauseating"

"Very well Edith" responds Charters.

"I must confess, I'm not altogether very surprised at this. I've always suspected that there was a shoddy streak in Sinclair's character" says the angry and dismayed Edith. She haughtily turns her nose up at Caldicott in disgust.

Caldicott sees how the situation must look and tries once more to clear his name in order to reclaim his reputation, "Listen, wait a minute" he starts to say.

Once again he is interrupted by Charters "You will hear more of this later Caldicott". He follows his sister's example in looking scornfully at the disgraced Caldicott, before they both leave the room.

Despondent, Caldicott says to himself "This is dreadful". Suddenly realising that the intruder is responsible for his troubles, he angrily demands "Okay, you must explain". Turning to face the young woman, he instantly realises that she is no longer there. "Where is she?" he murmurs to himself, looking around the room to locate her. Seeing the open window; he walks over to it and looks out. Not seeing her, he tries to remember the woman's name "La thing; Miss Whatsit" he shouts.

Caldicott is in his room brushing his hair with a brush in each hand, when he hears a knock on the door. "Come in" he says and turns to see the hotel manager enter.

Caldicott walks over to the Hotel manager who says "I am the Hotel Manager; I understand that you rang for me Mr Caldicott?"

"Yes, yes. Maybe rather an extraordinary thing to ask" says Caldicott as he nervously plays with the two hair brushes, "but could you tell me who occupies the room next door?"

"I can" replies the hotel manager, "Have they been annoying you sir?"

"Yes, err and no" stutters Caldicott with an embarrassed smile.

The Hotel manager folds his arms and strokes his chin as he thinks.

"Let me see?" he says, "Your next door neighbour is rather a big man with a small moustache. I think his name is Charters"

Caldicott smiles and says "No, no, no, not him; no he's my friend"

"Oh!" exclaims the hotel manager, "I beg your pardon.

"As a matter of fact, this is a lady" says Caldicott.

"Oh" responds the hotel manager nodding his head, with a certain degree of presumed enlightenment.

"Yes, err" chuckles Caldicott. "If you could help at all, she goes under the name of La Palermo. But that might not be her real name".

"No sir?" says the Hotel manager, "Can you describe her? Any clothes she wears? I might be able to help".

"It's rather difficult to say" says Caldicott, "I've very rarely seen her with any clothes on". "Oh!" he exclaims, embarrassed at what he's just said. "You see"

"So" says the bemused Hotel Manager.

Sheepishly, Caldicott replies "Yes. What I mean is, she's on the stage and dances and that sort of thing"

"Oh artists!" exclaims the Hotel manager, trying to be politely helpful, "Perhaps you could describe her face to me"

"Well" says Caldicott. "I've hardly noticed her. Of course she has a face and err eyes. Green eyes, I think they are; two of them; and long hair" as he indicates the back of his head with his hand. "Well, not very long, you know, it comes down half way. And a white throat, a very nice throat and she err sings out of, err through it; comes right through it". He knows that he hasn't described her very well; but after all, how does one describe a woman. The hotel manager smiles at his awkwardness and his feeble attempts to describe the woman intruder.

Caldicott notices Charters entering the room and greets him "Oh hello Charters", before turning back to the Hotel manager to say "Well manager, you'll try and trace this woman?"

The Hotel manager replies "I will sir; immediately" and bows his head before leaving the room.

Charters casually walks over to Caldicott, all the while playing with something small in his hands. He nods towards the manager who is just leaving the room and asks "What's he want?"

"I'm trying to find out some more about La Palermo" replies Caldicott Charters is still annoyed with his friend after the previous night's escapades and even more dismayed at Caldicott's attempts to try and contact the woman again. He curtly says "I should have thought that that was superfluous" as he hands Caldicott what he is holding in his hand. He explains, "Edith sends her ring back"

A stunned Caldicott asks "Is, is she calling it off?"

"Absolutely" replies his friend folding his arms resolutely. "She's grateful for one thing; she says she found out in time. Personally, I don't blame her. Its' not playing the game Caldicott. I can't put it stronger than that".

Caldicott is both disappointed with the news that his friend has brought but also annoyed that not only does his friend think bad of him, but Edith does too. How dare Charters accuse him of not playing the game. He responds to Charters in the only way that an English gentleman can behave when accused of something so terrible, and angrily says "I think that you are behaving in the most unbearable manner". He once again tries to explain exactly what happened the previous night; "I wake up, I find La Palermo haring about the bedroom"

Charters angrily interrupts by saying "You don't expect me to believe a story like that?"

Caldicott replies "I'm going to get this matter put straight if we have to stay in Budapest". He pauses to carefully think about what he is going to say next before continuing "Well, until we miss the Test Match".

Before Charters has a chance to challenge him again, there is a knock at the door.

"Come in" says Caldicott. It is the Hotel Manager; he says "Pardon; there is no one called La Palermo staying at this hotel. But I have just discovered there is a lady of the same name appearing at the Montana Cabaret tonight".

"Ah!" exclaims Caldicott, "That's her, there's no doubt about it. Thank you very much" As he finishes, the Hotel manager bows his head and leaves the room.

Throughout this conversation, Charters stands listening intently with his arms folded, showing his displeasure at this further turn of events. Unperturbed, Caldicott says "I'm going to find this woman Charters". Sternly, Charters replies "If you take my advice, you won't go near her".

Caldicott is still annoyed with his friend, for not only doubting his word on what did or did not happen the previous evening, but also because he appears unwilling to help him resolve the predicament that he finds himself in.

He snaps "I've taken your advice often enough. That woman has got to be made to explain to Edith. Come on, get dressed, we're going to the Montana".

Caldicott tries to explain why he had a young woman in his hotel room.

At this determination shown by his friend in the face of adversary and with his British stiff upper lip approach to the problem, Charters allows a slight smile to cross his face; his believe in Caldicott's innocence restored by this stirring speech, he is willing to help his friend to clear his name.

Return to your hotel immediately

A short time later, Charters and Caldicott, dressed in black tie and jacket, walk into the foyer of the Hotel Montana. The Maitre d' approaches them and greets them "Good evening Gentlemen". Charters respond with a "Good Evening" in return.
"A table for two sir?" asks the Maitre d'.
"We want to see La Palermo" says Caldicott
"Ah ah" says the Maitre d', "You'll be wanting front tables sir" and laughs.

Charters curtly replies "No, no", at which the Maitre'd' looks at him with a confused expression on his face. Charters doesn't respond other than nervously adjusts his tie.

Caldicott explains their requirements, "We don't want to see her perform, we want to see her privately"

Shaking his head, the Maitre d' says "Oh but I am afraid that is not possible. You see, the cabaret is just about to start" indicating the stage with his hand.

"Well, in that case, perhaps you could give her a note after the show" asks Charters.

"With pleasure sir" replies the Maitre d', "May I take you to your table?" Charters and Caldicott both say "Thank you" in unison and follow him.

Having ordered two whiskies, they arrive at the table moments just as the show starts. La Palermo is singing accompanied by a group of musicians dressed in their national folk costumes. As the two Englishmen watch and listen to her dancing and singing, Caldicott quietly says to Charters, "You know, watching her it is hard to believe that she's a thief".

Charters says nothing but stares intently at his friend.

Caldicott ignores his friend's intense stare and continues to watch La Palermo's performance. Not getting a reaction, Charters returns to enjoying his cigar whilst also observing the effect that La Palermo is having on his friend.

Caldicott smiles, or rather grins, as he realises what the next part of the performance will be. "She's warming up to the Take Off, old man" he says. Charters is not amused but before he has the opportunity to express his own thoughts, the Maitre d' arrives at the table carrying a tray. "Your whiskies gentlemen" he says as he places the tray on the table. A soda bottle accompanies the two glasses of whiskey. Before they have a chance to take a sip of whisky, the light goes out putting the cabaret room into total darkness.

"How extraordinary; whatever has happened Charters?" asks Caldicott. Before his friend can muster a reply, a woman's voice very quietly says "Don't touch the whisky, it is poisoned".

Within seconds, the lights have been switched back on and the Maitre d' crosses the room reassuring people "It's alright. It's alright Ladies and Gentlemen, it was only the switches. She will start again".

At this last comment the audience clap and cheer, glad that they haven't lost the opportunity to see and hear La Palermo dance and sing.

Unsure of what exactly he heard during the moments of darkness, Charters picks up his glass to taste his whisky and puts the glass to his mouth and breathes in the aroma. Before he takes a drink, Caldicott says "I say old man, look at this" reading a piece of paper he has found on the table in front of him.
"What does it say?" says Charters as he leans over to see what his friend is holding.
"This note" stutters Caldicott, "was put into my hand when the lights went out,
"Read it" he says and passes the note to his friend.
As Charters reads the note, his face changes to a look of horror. The note says;

> *Return to your hotel immediately.*
> *They are trying to steal that record of La Palermo.*
> *You must stop them.*
> *Be at St. Joseph's Baths at 11:00 am tomorrow*
> *Everything will be explained.*

This note, plus the whispered warning, gives Charters great cause for concern for their safety. He puts the whisky glass to his nose and smells; he quickly realises that something is wrong with it. He looks at Caldicott with grave concern on his face; his friend looks back equally concerned. As the two men look around the room, they see that the dancers are reaching the climax of the routine; beyond them they see the Maitre d' staring at them with what can only be described as evil malice on his face. Charters and Caldicott avert their eyes from him, not only because of his evil stare but primarily being English, they are both slightly embarrassed at being caught staring themselves.. Not knowing what to do next, they continue sitting in silence watching the dancers. They both have a strange feeling knowing that their lives are in danger, all they can do is sit there contemplating the situation and twiddle with their fingers, whilst all around, people continue to enjoy the evening's entertainment.

The dance finishes and Charters takes a quick look over at the Maitre d'; not knowing what else to say, says "Yes well". Caldicott also takes a quick look around the now empty dance floor and says nothing. Charters says "I think that we might as well be going now"
"It will look very silly" replies Caldicott, "we've only just come in"
They both glance over at the Maitre d' again; seeing that his attention has been diverted by his requirement to attend to another table, they see their opportunity to leave quickly. As they leave, Charters has a quick glance back to check whether their departure is noticed or not; it hasn't yet!

Back in the hotel, Charters and Caldicott are walking along the corridor towards their rooms when Caldicott says "You know, I'm not sure that we're not making awful fools of ourselves"
"What do you mean?" asks Charters.
"Well, dashing away from that place just because somebody put a note in our hand about the gramophone record" replies Caldicott.
"Have you got the key?" whispers Charters as they approach Caldicott's room.
"Yes, in my pocket" whispers back Caldicott and retrieves the key from his pocket. He turns to Charters and asks "What are we whispering for?".
"Sssh" says Charters looking behind him, "open the door quietly, there might be somebody inside". The whole situation has a strange feeling about it; his suspicions are raised to the extent that needs to be prepared for something nasty to happen at any moment. The two English men creep into the room as quietly as they can and switch on the light in order to surprise any intruder. They were right to be suspicious; switching the light comes on, they disturb an intruder.
"What's that" shouts Charters.
The intruder, a man, is startled but not enough to prevent him from leaping through the open window onto the balcony. As quickly as the man escapes, Charters and Caldicott rush across the room to the window. Charters is the first to arrive, he looks out of the window to see which direction the intruder goes. It is too late; he sees nothing of the intruder and turns to face Caldicott to say "He's gone".

Thinking quickly, Charters exclaims "The record! See if that has gone too"

"Wait a minute" replies Caldicott as he thinks. "After La whatist disappeared, what did I do with it?"

"How should I know?" retorts Charters.

"Oh, Oh, I've got it" replies Caldicott as he recalls where he had put it; "I put it down somewhere".

"But where?" urges Charters, frustrated with his friend's lack of urgency and clarity.

"I know" says Caldicott, "on a seat in the bathroom" crossing the room to where it is hidden.

Charters goes to follow and says "But it must be there still"

Caldicott returns with the record saying "It is, that's a bit of luck"; he closely inspects the record to see what all the fuss is about

Charters says "Let me look at it"

Unable to see anything special about it, he passes it to him. His friend takes the record out of its sleeve and they both study it closely.

Turning the record over, Charters says "It looks like an ordinary record to me. Let's try it".

"I don't see any point in playing it; after all the label speaks for itself; Every Time You Look At Me sung by La Palermo" says Caldicott also pointing to the words on the label as he reads it aloud.

"But the note says it was terribly important" says Charters

"Should we believe that?" queries Caldicott.

Why not?" remonstrates Charters, "Don't you realise that if all of this is true, then it means that someone is attempting to take our lives".

"That's absurd" says Caldicott.

"Anyway, let's try the record" says Charters and moves swiftly over to the gramophone player. Lifting the lid, he places the record on to the turntable; the music starts playing. It is La Palermo singing Every Time You Look At Me; the first lines goes "There's no need for lovely..."

"It's La Palermo" states Charters, pacing around the room carefully listening to the words being sung for the hint of a clue.

"Nothing very sinister about that" says Caldicott.

"No" agrees Charters.

The record continues playing and the two Englishmen listen intently; Caldicott says "She's got a very nice voice, I think" .Before he has the chance to comment further, La Palermo's singing is replaced by the voice of a man speaking in German, "Achtung, achtung".

Charters and Caldicott listen to La Palermo's record.

They look at each other in amazement then look at the record; the man's voice continues to be heard from the gramophone player.

"Good Lord!" exclaims Caldicott.

"Its German" says Charters.

"I only know three words of German" says Caldicott; "Heil, Swastika and Reichstag".

"Practically all I know myself" says Charters.

"It sounds to me that he is saying, that there are no more territorial claims in Europe" says Caldicott.

""Well, we'd better find out what it is all about" adds Charters, "Turn it on 30", pointing to the speed control on the gramophone player. He adds "We'll have to pick out what we can" and his friend alters the speed.

They replay and replay the record several times at the lower speed and also at the faster speed, starting from where the man first starts speaking "Achtung, achtung".

They try to piece together words into sentences and sentences into something meaningful, using their very limited knowledge of German. At last they think they have something and turn off the gramophone player. Caldicott sits down next to his friend and turns to wearily ask "Well, what do you make of all that?".

Charters takes a puff on his pipe and carefully studies the words written down on a piece of the hotel's writing paper; "Well my German is, apparently, not so good as I thought it was. I know what Achtung at the beginning means though. Yes, I saw it once on a gate. Achtung die dun. Beware the dog in English" he says with confidence before taking another puff on his pipe.

"What a peculiar thing to say" says Caldicott.

"I know" replies Charters sarcastically, "Its' some reference to some fellow called Abdul Memory"

"I gather that" snaps Caldicott, displeased with his friends humour.

"I also recognise the word Oil" continues Charters.

"What kind of oil?" asks Caldicott.

"What do you mean?" queries Charters.

"Well, I mean, there are all kinds of oil" states Caldicott.

"Charters is slightly exasperated with his friend's nit-picking and removes his pipe from his mouth, "Just Oil!" he snaps, "there was something about a pipeline and a lot of ammunition".

"Very mysterious" says Caldicott.

"Mmmm" agrees Charters, "One thing that emerges is that whatever, it is highly important".

"Yes" agrees Caldicott and sarcastically adds, "From your translation that is absolutely clear".

Charters picks up on this comment with its sarcastic emphasis on his translation and turns to glare at Caldicott. Caldicott continues to speak, "Oh, by the way, didn't that note say something about being at St Joseph's Baths at 11 O'clock tomorrow morning?"

"Yes" his friend agrees.

"Oh well, we'd better go and see what it is all about?" says Caldicott.

"Mmm, you are probably right" agrees Charters, "In the meantime, I shall hide that record where nobody can find it".

Made a big splash!

The next morning, Charters and Caldicott make their way to St Joseph's baths with plenty of time to spare and time to get changed ready to use the baths. Not wanting to look out of place, they have the splendid idea of passing themselves off as bathers. Both wear matching striped towelling robes, provided as part of their entrance fee, they sit at a table just beside one of the pools in order to better see the comings and goings of the baths customers and whoever left them the note on the previous evening.

"I say Charters, look at that girl on the other side" says Caldicott nodding his head to indicate the girl he means. As Charters looks, Caldicott adds "A wonderful figure".

Shocked by what his friend has just said and the inappropriateness of it, Charters does a double take at the girl before frowning a look of disapproval at Caldicott.

"Nothing to be compared with Edith of course" Caldicott diplomatically adds, sensing his friend's displeasure.

"Made a big splash" says Charters as the girl dives into the pool.

"Oh I wouldn't say that" disagrees Caldicott, "She's a very good swimmer".

"Good Heavens!" exclaims Caldicott as he looks across the pool and sees a face that he recognises, "I believe; it can't be. Yes it is".

"What?" asks Charters.

"La Whatsit" says Caldicott as he realises it is La Palermo swimming across the pool to them.

"Caldicott" snaps Charters as he realises something very important and grabs his friend's arm, "She's probably behind this you know".

"What" queries Caldicott.

"Well I mean, La Palermo. She's shadowing us to find out where we left that record" says Charters.

"Well, it's quite obvious that we haven't got it on us now" says Caldicott all matter of fact, referring to their limited apparel and lack of hiding places.

"Sssh" says Charters, "She's climbing out, be careful".

La Palermo climbs out of the pool directly in front of the two Englishmen and picks up her towel which is lying at the edge of the pool. "Good morning" she says as she dries herself.

Charters and Caldicott, being English gentlemen, both stand and reply "Good morning".

"Is this chair free?" she asks.

"Yes, rather, sit down" replies Caldicott; all a little too eagerly for Charters liking.

"Thank you" she replies.

Given the relationship of his sister with his friend, and the woman being the reason for Edith breaking off the engagement, Charters is really not happy about this meeting between Caldicott and La Palermo,. He is also uncomfortable about them meeting a woman in the public baths, particularly when none of them are dressed entirely appropriately. He thinks it all rather unsavoury and says "As a matter of fact, we were just going"; he touches Caldicott on the arm and adds "Come on Caldicott"

"I think you'd better stay" says La Palermo as Charters starts to walk away, "Sit down" she insists
Charters and Caldicott oblige with La Palermo's request after looking at each other with a little trepidation.

Charters and Caldicott wait at St Joseph's baths.

La Palermo leans forward and asks "Do you remember the voice in the dark last night saying 'Don't drink that whisky, its' poisoned'?"

141

"Good heavens!" exclaims Caldicott as he looks at Charter who whispers "Was that you?"

"And on the telephone in Istanbul" adds La Palermo.

"That was you too?" asks Charters seeing a pattern emerge.

"Yes" replies la Palermo.

"Well that's astounding" adds Caldicott.

"I'm sorry if I've been a nuisance, but it was necessary" says La Palermo, "You see, I'm working for the British Secret Service"

"Do you see Caldicott" says Charters, "That explains all this funny business; espionage".

"And we're mixed up in it?" asks Caldicott.

"Yes" replies La Palermo.

"How?" enquires Charters.

"Well, because of the gramophone record" explains La Palermo, "It contains the details of the sabotage scheme in the Middle East". She looks at Caldicott and asks "Where is it now?"

Caldicott gives the question some careful thought before replying; after looking at his friend he says "Charters, where is it?"

"Oh, Oh" mutters Charters, "I've hidden it in a very cunning place in the hotel".

"Would you two do something for me?" asks La Palermo.

Caldicott is keen as mustard to help La Palermo and replies "Yes, rather".

Before he can say anything else, Charters grabs his friend's arm and says "Caldicott, wait a minute". He looks intensely at La Palermo and asks "What is it?"

La Palermo returns Charters stare and replies "I want you to take the record to the Traveller's Club and ask for a Captain Spanswick".

Charters recognises the name, "Spanswick" he says looking at Caldicott, "Not E.J.K. Spanswick who used to play cricket for Gloucester?"

"Yes" replies a smiling La Palermo.

"Good Lord!" excitedly exclaims Charters. He knows the name and cricketing reputation of the man.

"Good Gracious me!" exclaims the equally excited Caldicott, before adding "Yes well, yes".

"He's been sent by the British Intelligence to collect the record and take it back to London" explains La Palermo..

"And you want us to deliver it?" asks the still excited Charters

"Yes" replies La Palermo, "You simply have to say that Miss Deering sent you".

"What do you say Charters?" asks Caldicott.

Charters blushes as he realises that he needs to check his excitement and give the matter some considered thought; he finally says "Well" whilst he thinks.

La Palermo continues while he is thinking and says "That's all you have to do. Deliver it and then you can go on with your holiday in peace".

"Well, in that case" says Charters seemingly approving his involvement in the scheme.

"Thank you" says La Palermo, with a beaming smile on her face, "I knew that you'd help me. Captain Spanswick will be at the Travellers Club at 1 O'clock".

"Do you mean today?" asks Charters

"Yes" she replies, "You are to go right away. Goodbye, thank you".

Before it gets to the German stuff

Back in the hotel foyer, Charters and Caldicott are dressed in their usual attire of suits with collar and tie. As they walk across the foyer, Caldicott turns to Charters and asks "Are you certain that you remember where you put the record?".

"Yes, yes" replies his friend, "I found the perfect place".

"Where?" asks Caldicott.

"Amongst the other records in the dining room" says Charters.

"But you'll never find it" says a concerned Caldicott.

Charters is amused at his friend's lack of confidence in him and laughs as he taps his friend on the shoulder to indicate that he wants him to follow him to the dining room. "I know exactly where it is old man" says the chuckling Charters; "Fifteen from the end".

"Oh" says Caldicott as they walk past the reception desk towards the dining room and to where the record is hidden.

Before they get there, they hear La Palermo's voice coming from the dining room. "Do you hear that?" asks Caldicott.

"It's her song" says Charters.

"Her voice too" adds the alarmed Caldicott.

Charters claps his head as he suddenly realises something very important and shouts "It's the record!"

"Quick" says Caldicott, "before it gets to the German stuff". They both rush to the dining room. It being midday it is very busy and full of diners; Charters and Caldicott find it difficult to move quickly through the packed dining room. Caldicott bumps into one of the waiters, knocking the tray that he was carrying, crashing to the floor with a loud bang. This doesn't stop them though, they carry on rushing through the dining room bumping into more diners, tables and chairs, causing quite a scene as they crash their way through. Unbeknown to them, Charters' sister is amongst the diners, sitting at one of the tables. Hearing a disturbance, she stands like many of the other diners in order to see what all the fuss is about. Seeing exactly who is causing the commotion, she stands with arms folded, deeply disturbed and alarmed at the unseemly behaviour of her brother and her fiancée and the chaos that they are causing. For once, she is lost for words.

Charters gets to the record player first, fortunately La Palermo's voice is still being heard and not the voice of the man with the secret message in German. He pulls the arm across the turntable, scratching the record in the process; the volume of record player was on high, so the diners hear the scratch but they certainly don't hear the secret message.
Unfortunately, Caldicott doesn't fare too well in racing across the dining room, what with many of the diners standing to try and get a better view of the proceedings. He crashes into diner after diner, before crashing into a table and falls into a heap on the floor covered in flowers and napkins. Dazed, he looks up to see Charters at the record player waving the record triumphantly, almost as if he had won first prize in a race or something similar. Adding to this image, he hears Charters shouting "Caldicott, I've got it, I've got it Caldicott". Like himself, he notices that Charters is also smeared with food; for which he sees him wiping food from his face.

Having recovered the record and cleaned themselves, Charters and Caldicott arrive at The Traveller's Club. The two Englishmen follow the waiter through the club; "This is it old man" says Charters.
"Well what do we do when we meet him?" asks Caldicott.
"Give him the record I suppose" replies Charters.
Approaching the bottom of the stairs, Caldicott turns to Charters and thoughtfully says "I do think that we ought to be extremely guarded".

"Yes" says Charters nodding in agreement with his friend's considered approach to the risky business of espionage.

They continue following the waiter up the stairs to where they are shown into a room where a man, presumably Captain Spanswick stands to greet them.
"Oh! Captain Spanswick?" Charters asks as he goes to shake the man's hand.

Captain Spanswick puts his hand out to greet Charters and says "In the flesh".
"My name is Charters" says Charters introducing himself.
"I'm Caldicott" adds his friend.
"How do you do?" comes the reply.
"How do you do" says Caldicott to Captain Spanswick.
Caught up in the excitement, Charters also says "How do you do" but confusingly to Caldicott. All three men chuckle at the amusing situation.

Charters begins to explain the reason for their visit, "We are friends of Miss Deering".
"So I understand" says Captain Spanswick, "Sit down won't you"
"Thank you very much" says Charters as he and Caldicott sit.
"And how is Miss Deering?" asks Captain Spanswick.
"Well" says Charters, "The last time we saw her, she was getting along swimmingly".
"If you follow our meaning" adds Caldicott with a smile.
Captain Spanswick returns the smile and says "I rather think I do".
"You'll be glad to hear that we have the err, consignment of wax" explains Caldicott somewhat confusingly.
"I beg your pardon?" asks the confused Captain Spanswick.

Charters steps in to try and better explain what his friend means but follows Caldicott's lead in being guarded; "The sample disk" he says, "for you to take to your firm".
"Oh, you mean that gramophone record" says the now enlightened Captain.
"Sssh" says Charters as he looks suspiciously around the room.
"Somebody might hear" adds Caldicott.
"Oh we are alright here" explains the Captain, "Well where is it?".

"Under Caldicott's coat" explains Charters, "I suggest he slips it under the chair. You can take it away when we've gone".

"There's no point in being furtive" says Captain Spanswick, "Someone always notices if you are. I'll take it now" and he puts out his hand to take the record from Caldicott.

Charters and Caldicott look at each other with trepidation. "What, just like that?" asks Caldicott.

"Why not?" replies the Captain.

"In that case" says Caldicott, "Here you are" and takes the record from under his jacket and puts it in the Captain's outstretched hand.

"Thanks old man" says the Captain.

"I don't mind telling you that we are very glad to be getting it out of our hands" says Caldicott very relieved.

"Yes" adds Charters, chuckling with a hint of relieve in his voice.

Captain Spanswick stands and says "Congratulations, you fellows have put up a jolly good show".

"Oh very nice of you to say so" says Caldicott.

Charters smiles and nods in agreement; "Well we happen to do our best, you know".

"By the way" asks Captain Spanswick, "Have you heard this record?"

"Yes" replies Charters, "Yes, as a matter of fact we have".

"Then you know it's' contents?" asks the Captain.

"Well more or less you know; more or less" replies Charters.

"It's in German" adds Caldicott.

"The Captain looks very concerned at what he is hearing and murmurs something indistinguishable to the others.

"I have a fair command of the language" says Charters, "I gather it refers to some kind of do in the Middle East".

"Oil" adds Caldicott.

""Yes, that's right" agrees Charters.

"And I believe that there is a dog in it somewhere too" adds Caldicott,

"Well, yes, possibly" interrupts Charters, having less confidence in his interpretation skills than his friend does.

"I'm leaving for England with this tonight" says the Captain holding the record. Impressed, Charters says "Ooh, Well then, you'll be in time for the last West Indies Test Match. We, we hope to get there too". He smiles and turns to look at his friend who is also smiling at the thought of getting back to England to watch the Test Match.

"Yes, as a matter of fact" says Caldicott "but Charters and I are great admirers of yours".

"Yes, rather" agrees Charters.

"We were in a stand at Lords in 1929 when you played against Middlesex" explains Caldicott.

Captain Spanswick is listening intently to what the two gentlemen are saying; "Middlesex?" he asks.

"Yes, you carried the bat for seventy five including two magnificent swipes for six" chuckles Charters at the thought of the cracking game he had the pleasure of witnessing. "Ha-ha" he laughs, "one of them landed in our stand".

"It was Charters who threw the ball back" explains Caldicott.

"Yes" confirms Charters. "I don't suppose you remember that though?" he asks.

"I'm afraid I don't follow" says the confused Captain Spanswick.

Charters says "You are E.J.K., aren't you?"

"E.J.K.?" asks the Captain.

"Yes!" says Caldicott, "Spanswick the cricketer"

""No" replies the Captain.

This reply disheartens Charters, "oh" he says.

"I don't play cricket" explains the Captain.

Charters and Caldicott look at each other, aghast at what they have just heard and simultaneously retort "Don't play cricket!"

At that moment, there is a knock on the door and all three men turn to look to see who enters.

The waiter walks in and says "excuse me sir"; he looks at Charters and Caldicott and asks "Mr Charters, Mr Caldicott?"

"That's right" replies Charters.

"You are wanted on the phone at once. An urgent call" the waiter says.

"Eh?" queries Caldicott.

"What an extraordinary thing" says Charters, looking at the Captain, in the hope that he has an explanation. None comes so he adds "Excuse us Mr Spanswick".

"Certainly" the Captain replies.

Charters and Caldicott follow the waiter out of the room and continue following him down the stairs.

"I wonder who it can be" asks Caldicott.

Equally puzzled, his friend replies "I don't know"

In the reception area, the waiter opens a door into an office and says "At the desk sir. I'll stay by the door".

Caldicott sits at the desk and picks up the receiver, "Hello, yes, who's there?"

He hears the reply "La Palermo; Miss Deering". It is La Palermo and she continues to say "Listen to me. You must not meet Captain Spanswick. Do you understand?"

"But we've already met him" explains Caldicott.

"Then leave quickly. Whatever you do, don't give him the record" she says.

"Ha-ha, I'm afraid he's already got it" says Caldicott

"Listen to me" says La Palermo, "the man you've just met is an imposter. Captain Spanswick's body was found in the Danube this morning.

At this news, Caldicott's face changes from smiling at the thought of talking to La Palermo to shock at being betrayed and also shock at the death of the real Captain Spanswick; "Good heavens!" he exclaims.

La Palermo shouts down the phone "You must get that record back, you must. Do you understand?"

Realising the significance of what he has just been told, he replies "Alright, we'll try. Hold on". He turns to face Charters who asks "What's all the fuss about?"

"Spanswick is dead" explains Caldicott.

"But he can't be, we've just seen him" says Charters, surprised at his friend's news.

Caldicott tries to explain further, "Spanswick is not Spanswick; he's a fraud"

"Hold on, I'll go and catch him" whispers Charters as he rushes out of the office leaving Caldicott alone sitting at the desk.

Caldicott returns the receiver to his ear and confusingly says "La dear, Miss Whatsit"

"Listen" she screams back down the phone, "I can't hold on any longer. He's seen me. He's coming towards me. Mr Caldicott, they've caught me. Get that record back whatever you do" She breaks off with along terrifying scream before the line goes suddenly dead..

Caldicott tries in vain to talk to her again, "Hello, Hello" pressing the receiver switch several times in the hope that it is just a faulty connection; but all to no avail as he can't reconnect with her.

He presses again to get the operator and says "Hello, is that the operator? I've been cut off, can you trace that call? "

Before he gets a response to his call for assistance, Charters reappears in the doorway and says "I say old boy, the fellow's gone, so has the record"

"So has she old man" says Caldicott with the receiver still to his ear.

"Who?" asks Charters.

"La dear, Miss Palermo" says Caldicott replies, "Its' most extraordinary"

Caldicott hears the operator talking to him, "Hello" he says to her, "yes" he adds before asking "where?"

"Oh, thank you" he finally says and puts down the receiver. He turns to Charters and says "I say, that, that's very odd"

"What?" asks Charters.

"She was phoning from a public call box at the Central Station and she suddenly shouted 'He's coming towards me', screamed and then she was cut off"

Charters asks "Did she say who was coming towards her?"

"No" replies Caldicott.

"But how could whoever it was, be coming towards her in the telephone box" asks Charters, confused at what he has just heard.

"It's beyond ne" replies Caldicott and stands to try and understand exactly what has happened; "First she says give the record to Spanswick, then she say that Spanswick is floating down the Danube"

Charters interrupts by adding "Then she screams that someone is coming towards her and cuts off. Why?"

"Perhaps he pushed her against Button B" suggests Caldicott, without any hint of irony.

Charters murmurs; he is not so sure about this last bit and asks "What are we going to do about it?"

"I tell you what" suggests Caldicott, "Let's go back to the hotel, have a couple of drinks and talk about it"

"A good idea" agrees Charters, "I could do with one, in fact several".

Schwarzoff Castle

Later, back in the bar at the Hotel, Charters and Caldicott drink whisky; after a couple of sips Caldicott is feeling more relaxed and says "Well I feel better now"

"Yes" agrees Charters, "now let's review the situation"

149

"Do you suppose it will be any good if we told our story to the British Consul?" asks Caldicott.

"Oh, Oh they'll never believe it" replies Charters.

"We could leave out all the ridiculous bits" suggests Caldicott.

"There wouldn't be much left" says Charters thinking that the whole thing sounds so farfetched that nobody in their right mind would believe them.

"Well, what else can we do?" asks his friend.

As they think through their options and continue sipping their whisky, they are approached by a hotel concierge who says "Excuse me gentlemen"

"Yes" acknowledges Charters.

"A Miss Kronowski is asking for you.

""Kronowski, Kronowski" murmurs Charters as he tries to place the name, "I don't know a Kronowski; do you?" he asks Caldicott.

"No" his friend replies.

"She is standing over there" says the concierge indicating towards the hotel reception desk where they see a woman. Based on the style of clothing she is wearing, they presume that she is a native Hungarian. Charters and Caldicott, intrigued, walk over towards the woman.

"Good afternoon" says Charters greeting her.

The young woman curtsies politely and enquires "Mr Charters, Mr Caldicott?".

"That's right" says Charters

"I sell chocolate on the Central Station" she explains.

"Oh, oh, that's very nice for you" says Charters interrupting her.

"This afternoon" she continues, "a lady, she lean out of the train window to buy a packet of chocolate. She gave me a hundred Pengo with this note" and taps the note before passing it to Charters.

"Oh" says Charters surprised at being given the note. He reads the envelope and sees that it is addressed to Messers Charters and Caldicott, The Carnegie Hotel, "Yes, well, thank you very much" he says to Miss Kronowski and takes a small amount of money from his pocket to pass to her, "Here's something for your trouble.

She looks at the money that Charters has given her and gives a big smile, pleased about being given another generous tip. "Thank you" she says , curtsies again and quickly leaves the hotel.

"Central Station?" queries Caldicott, "It must be from her, quick, open it".

Charters puts his cigarette into his mouth so that he can use both hands to open the envelope. "La Palermo" he says as he sees that the envelope contains a photo of the singer.

"Yes" says a grinning Caldicott, "obviously taken at the end of her dance" and turns the photo over to see a message written on the back. "What does this mean, Schwarzoff, Crimalberg, SOS?"

"SOS?" queries Charters, "it's a cry of distress old man"

"Yes" agrees Caldicott, "but Schwarzoff, Crimalberg?"

"Probably some sort of address she wants us to go to, we'll ask at the desk".suggests Charters

They both approach the hotel reception desk where Charters asks "Oh I say".

"Yes sir" the receptionist replies.

"Do you know where Schwarzoff, Crimalberg is?", not exactly confident of what he is asking.

"Crimalberg" says the receptionist, "that's a town near the Hungarian border sir, but I do not know Schwarzoff"

"Oh!" exclaims Caldicott.

Looking at Caldicott, the receptionist suggests "Perhaps the guide book will help you. I have one, one moment" as she turns to find the guide book on the shelf behind her.

"Hey" says Charters to Caldicott, "I don't think we ought to do anything hasty. I mean we don't want to start out on a wild goose chase"

"It's not a goose old man" says Caldicott, "but an owl"

Before Charters has a chance to respond to Caldicott's poor taste in humour and the timing of it, the hotel receptionist returns with the guide book. "Here we are" she says, "Crimalberg; page 47" smiling as she passes the guide book to Caldicott.

"Thanks" says Caldicott and starts to read the guide book.

"Here we are, Crimalberg" he says, just then something catches his eye and he exclaims "I say Charters, here it is" pointing to the page.

"What?" asks Charters.

"On the summit of which is the Schwarzoff, a 15th century castle, formerly the residence of Count Elongey"

He immediately turns back to the receptionist and asks "What time does the train leave for Crimalberg?"

"I'll look them up" she replies helpfully.

At that very moment, the two Englishmen hear a shrill, but very familiar voice, shouting "Sinclair!, Hawtrey!".
Immediately a look of alarm appears on the faces of Charters and Caldicott as they recognise the voice belonging to Edith. They look at each and slowly turn round to where Edith is standing to see her looking sterner than ever.
"So you're back" she snaps.
"Hello Edith" Caldicott nervously says.

The Hotel Receptionist (Patricia Medina) helps Charters to find the location of Crimalberg and Schwarzoff Castle.

Following the events of the previous evening, Edith ignores Caldicott's greeting but says "Whenever I see you two lately, you give me a haunted look, mumble on about a lot of balderdash and rush off like a couple of rabbits.

152

Charters and Caldicott don't know what to say to this accusation, so stand there nervously looking at each other as if guilty as charged. Charters is the first to speak, "Oh really Edith"

Edith cuts him off with a withering look before he can say anything and asks "I suppose that it will be too much to ask for an explanation; always supposing that there is one?"

"Oh yes, yes, rather, mmm" stutters Charters, "There's an explanation alright"

"Just at the moment, we can't think what it is" interjects Caldicott.

"Sinclair" Edith snaps, eying the photograph of La Palermo that Caldicott has in his hand, "Who's that photograph off that you are holding in your hands? It's that woman. Give it to me this minute" and reaches out to take the photo from Caldicott.

Caldicott is too quick for her and puts his hand and the photograph behind his back out of Edith's reach. "I can't do that Edith, because there's err something written on the other side"

"No doubt" retorts Edith, thinking the worse of Caldicott..

"I agree it looks pretty bad but err" stutters Charters as he tries to explain.

"There's no need for it Hawtrey, I shall speak to Mother about you when I get back" she icily says looking directly at Charters. She turns to face Caldicott and adds "As for you Sinclair, I shall visit your Grandfather at Bishop Storford and lay the whole matter before him"

Caldicott is distraught at the thought of his Grandfather hearing a tale of woe from his fiancée; he is defeated and lost for words. However, Charters has had enough and leaps to his friend's defence; he asks "My good woman, what's his Grandfather got to do with this?"

Before Edith has a chance to reply, the hotel receptionist who has been watching the discussion patiently waiting for an opportunity to speak says "Excuse me gentlemen, there's a train leaving for Crimalberg in a quarter of an hour"

"What time is the next one?" asks Caldicott.

"Not until this evening" she replies.

Caldicott looks at his watch as Charters says "We can't wait until then".

"Fifteen minutes, we can just make it" says Caldicott.

"Yes of course we can" agrees Charters excitedly.

The two men rush off past Edith without giving any explanation and leave her standing there even more annoyed than before. "Sinclair, Hawtrey, come back" she loudly demands; all to no avail as by this time, Charters and Caldicott are running up the stairs to collect their coats.

Neither of them stop but Charters shouts back, "Can't stop now old girl!"

"We'll explain later" Caldicott adds.

Edith is not satisfied at all, she shouts with a level of venom and anger in her voice that even she as an English woman is not entirely sure is appropriate, "You won't have the opportunity. After this, I'm returning to England at once; do you hear?" all to no avail once more.

Having rushed from the hotel to the railway station, Charters and Caldicott manage to catch the train. The journey takes them from Budapest across Hungary to Crimalberg. On arriving at Crimalberg, the two Englishmen plan how they will approach the castle. Their plan relies on them not being seen if at all possible. To accomplish this, they decide to enter the castle, not via the easy way along the road, but by climbing up the mountain to the castle. Eventually, and without too many problems, Charters and Caldicott complete their weary climb, and finally drop down from the castle wall into a small enclosed courtyard.

"Aaah" sighs Charters wearily as he uses his handkerchief to mop his brow. Caldicott is brushing the dust from his jacket and trousers. Looking around, he sees an opportunity and whispers "A window that's open over there". Charters looks to where Caldicott his indicating and replies "Yes, yes. It looks like it, yes. I say, they are asking to be burgled aren't they?"

Caldicott looks at his friend in amusement and wryly says "They are going to be. Come on" and taps Charters on the shoulder indicating him to follow.

Quietly and swiftly, they make their way across the courtyard to just below the open window. An ivy vine has grown all the way up the side of the building; looking at each other, they nod and silently agree that this is their route to the open window. They take one last look around to make sure that they have not been spotted.

As they are about to start climbing, Charters has a quick thought, "La Paloma had better be here when we get inside"

"I hope she realises what we are doing for her" adds Caldicott.

154

Side by side, the two English men climb the ivy clinging to the side of the castle building, until they finally reach the open window. Without making the slightest sound, they clamber through the opening into the darkened room. Eventually, their eyes become accustomed to the dimness and they see that the room is sparsely furnished, giving them some confidence that it is a room not often used. "It all seems very easy" says Charters

"Sssh" says Caldicott, hearing a very familiar voice coming from beyond the closed door. "Hear that" he says, "La Palermo" as he hears her familiar voice singing the song they have heard so recently.

"Yes" whispers Charters in agreement.

Very quietly, they slowly push open the door which opens into a much larger and lit room than the one they are in. "Ssh" whispers Charters, "somebody's coming". Silently, they move across the room to where they see a pair of curtains extending from the ceiling right down to the floor; an ideal place for them to quickly hide. It is dark behind and shuffling into the enveloping darkness, they stumble across something to rest on whilst they hide. Their timing is impeccable, within seconds of hiding they hear somebody entering the room and switch on the lights. They sit there, as quite as mice, listening to the soft footsteps crossing the room. All of a sudden, the curtains are opened with a swish, dazzling the two men and exposing them from their hiding place. Shocked and dazed, Charters and Caldicott freeze to the spot, revealed in the newly lit room. The seat that they found in the darkness is also revealed; it is a large chair and both Charters and Caldicott remain seated and squashed together between the two arms of the large chair, looking a little like two naughty schoolboys caught red-handed at some boyish prank.

The person who opened the curtain, doesn't smile at this funny sight in front of them; it is a servant who is probably used to seeing this sort of behaviour from his own masters. He politely bows and formally says "Good evening gentlemen. Mr Charters and Mr Caldicott, I presume?" Sheepishly, Charters and Caldicott remain seated; Charters nods and quietly replies "Yes".

Caldicott adds "Yes, that's right"

Without a hint of sarcasm or humour, the manservant says "I beg your pardon for disturbing you, but I understood the two of you were in here, and seeing your feet protruding from under the curtains, I took the liberty of drawing them"

155

Charters and Caldicott are even more embarrassed at this humiliating way that that they were caught; they both look sheepishly at their feet. "Oh" says Caldicott and trying to gain some composure, he stands to greet their greeter, "Very kind of you"

The servant (Charles Rolfe) find Charters and Caldicott hiding behind the curtain

They follow the servant across the room who says "You are a little later than we expected"
"Yes" replies Caldicott, "err what" he adds as he realises the implications of what has just been said to them. Not knowing quite what to say or how to respond he stutters "oh, err, what, you see" without actually saying anything in particular.
Reaching the other side of the room, the servant raises the lid of the gramophone player and stops the music. Caldicott tries to provide a reason for their presence inside the castle and says, "We were, err, in the neighbourhood and we thought that we would just pop in and have a look around the castle"

Charters nervously chuckles. The servant turns to look at them with a big knowing smile on his face.

"I agree, it is a wonderful old place isn't it" adds Charters following his friend's lead.

"Fifteenth century sir" explains the servant.

"Is it really?" asks Caldicott, "well I, err, don't think that there is anything to keep us any longer is there Charters?"

Charters takes his hat off and chuckles, "No, I don't think so"

"Just a minute sir, I believe you are dining with my master" says the servant.

Charters and Caldicott are rather taken aback and look at each other with a certain level of alarm. Uncertain as to how to react, they mumble to each other before Charters enquires "Master?"

"Yes sir" comes the reply.

"Phew, how extraordinarily decent of him" says Charters, "Yes, yes, I'm very surprised. As a matter of fact, we have another appointment"

"I don't think you have sir" says the servant firmly but with a polite smile.

Good heavens!

Just then, a curtain is pulled back to reveal Captain Spanswick dressed differently from when they last met him. This time he is wearing a German officer's dress uniform. "Aaah, Good Evening gentlemen" he says to greet them.

"Good heavens!" exclaims Charters, shocked at the turn of events.

"Captain Spanswick" says Caldicott, equally shocked.

Now that his master, Captain Spanswick has arrived to greet the guests, the servant leaves. Captain Spanswick, now revealed as a German Officer, by the way of an explanation says "Captain Spanswick has no doubt had his just desserts and is unfortunately dead. I ventured to take his place when you came to the Traveller's Club"

"Yes and you took that record too" roars Charters accusingly, "What have you done with it?"

"And what have you done with Miss thingy?" demands Caldicott.

"She will be here in a moment" replies the phoney Spanswick, "May I introduce myself. I am Max Bauer and I work quite hard for the German Intelligence service. I figure in their records in the sensational ways that secret services have as K7"

Charters and Caldicott confront the German secret agent Max Bauer (Cyril Gardner)

Charters turns to Caldicott and says "I always said that we should have gone to the British Consul"

Riled, Caldicott snaps "Look here, if you think we are going to stay here and have dinner with you, you are sadly mistaken"

"Yes" agrees Charters.

Max Bauer does not immediately respond but coolly picks up a cigarette box from the table.

"We are leaving at once" says Caldicott, determined more than ever to bring the matter to a satisfactory conclusion.

"I don't think so Mr Caldicott" coldly says Max Bauer, "in fact to be brutally frank, I am very much afraid that neither of you will leave here at all; ever!"

"Eh, what?" asks Caldicott with shock.

Charters realise the significance of what has just been said and quietly asks "You mean, we are going to be killed?"

"It is a political necessity" explains Max Bauer.

"But that will be murder" retorts Charters

"I regret the necessity, almost as you do" says Max Bauer very matter of factly. He offers cigarettes to the two Englishmen, who are now his prisoners.

Taking one, Caldicott asks "Haven't you got hold of the wrong end of the stick?"

"How do you mean?" asks Max Bauer as he proffers a light to the cigarette that Charters has accepted.

"Well, we're not British agents or anything like that" says Caldicott.

"Oh quite" acknowledges Max Bauer, "but you told me yourselves at The Traveller's Club in Budapest that this record refers to a sabotage scheme of ours in the Middle East not unconnected with oil"

"Did we?" asks Caldicott.

"Hey, interjects Charters, "we all make mistakes you know"

"Yes" adds Caldicott, "especially Charters where he tries to translate German.

"Oh rather" agrees a smiling and bemused Charters, "I hardly know that 'nein' means 'yes'"

"Indeed" agrees Max Bauer, "nevertheless, you will understand that we are not anxious for Britain to know the details of our scheme; especially with the attack on your pipeline timed for midnight tomorrow"

Charters and Caldicott look at each with great consternation written across their faces. "Our pipeline?" demands Charters with anger.

"Midnight tomorrow?" demands an equally angry Caldicott

"So that's it" says Charters, finally realising what the secret message actually means.

"Really Mr K what you called, I've seldom heard of a dirtier piece of work" says Caldicott.

"Hear, hear" agrees his friend.

"Quite" agrees Bauer, "but you see my difficulty, I dare not allow even a hint of our plans to leak out"

"But, look here" reasons Caldicott, "couldn't we be merely imprisoned until it is all over?", to which Charters nods in agreement.

"Being men of honour, you would no doubt attempt to escape" explains Bauer.

"Naturally" says Charters

"After all, it is our pipeline" adds Caldicott in agreement.

"Well, there you are Gentlemen. You compel me to take care of you" explains Bauer.

Feeling tricked, yet again, Charters and Caldicott look at each other knowing that they have just signed their own death sentence with their foolish talk.

"And now" continues Bauer, "do let us have dinner" and leads the way to the dining room beyond a curtained doorway. The two Englishmen start to follow him, but stop in the doorway to take in the view of the dining table all set for dinner.

"I don't think I'm very hungry" says Charters.

"The food's poisoned of course" suggests Caldicott.

"Oh yes" agrees his friend.

Hearing these comments, Max Bauer turns to say, "My dear Mr Caldicott, I assure you, you can eat without the slightest misgiving"

"Oh well in that case" suggests Charters quickly recovering his appetite.

"After you gentlemen" indicates Bauer, "you know it is such a pity. You are good fellows; I can see that"

"It's' very nice of you to say so" says Caldicott, sitting down at the table.

"I was really sorry that all of this has happened" says Bauer, turning to his servant to pass him the cigarette box. "You can serve dinner right away" he instructs him.

Dinner is served and sometime later finished, with little, other than polite conversation, passing between the three gentlemen. As dinner finishes, Bauer asks "A little more port Charters?".

Charters replies "Oh, thank you" Max Bauer continues with the discussion about the English men's holiday, "Yes it's a tragic tale. There you both were enjoying your holiday"

"Oh, just a second please" interrupts Caldicott, "do you mind if we stick to the present tense; after all we are still, just"

"Oh I do beg your pardon" apologies Bauer, "but through no fault of your own, you stumble into this affair and I, err, find the whole thing very disturbing"

"So do we as a matter of fact" agrees Charters puffing on a fine cigar provided by his captor.

"We understand your problem though" says Caldicott.

"Do let us change the subject" asks Bauer.

"Yes" agrees Charters, "excellent port you've got here" as he takes a sip.

"We take a pride in our cellar" explains Bauer, maintaining the polite dinner conversation.

A knock on the door interrupts the proceedings, all three turn to face the door. "Come in" says Bauer and the three gentlemen stand to greet the visitor. It is La Palermo accompanied with another man.
"Ah, come in, both of you" says Bauer to the two visitors, "I think you know these gentlemen Rand Gas"
"Yes, I think I do" acknowledges Rand Gas.
Bauer continues with the introductions, "And so I think does Miss Deering?". She apologetically replies "Yes, I'm terribly sorry about this".
"Oh, that's alright" says Caldicott, "you couldn't help it", by way of reassuring her that she's not to blame for their predicament.
"Miss Deering is leaving in the morning for Berlin" explains Bauer.
"I say" interrupts a concerned Caldicott, "You can't send her there"
Bauer doesn't comment on what Caldicott has just said, but continues with his explanation of what will happen to his guests; "An officer and a party of men will arrive here by plane during the night to collect her. They will attend to you before they leave"
"Oh!" exclaims Charters, "may I ask how", I mean, by what method?"
"It is painful to me to discuss it" says Bauer, "but I imagine that they will shoot you in the courtyard"
Crestfallen but not completely down, Caldicott sarcastically says "Oh, not in the heart. Thank you".
Ignoring Caldicott's attempt at humour, Bauer says "Well gentlemen, perhaps you'd like to get a little sleep. I have had my own room prepared for you"
"Awfully decent of you" says Charters, forever the polite English man.
"I could hardly do less" replies Bauer who turns to his servant, "Hogan, show these gentlemen to their room".
"Yes sir" replies Hogan the servant, looking at Charters and Caldicott and adding, "This way gentleman".
Before they leave the room, Caldicott turns to Miss Deering and says "Well Miss Deering, I suppose that we'd better say goodbye. I don't expect you'll be getting up to see us off"
She can't bear the thought of looking at Caldicott after all the trouble that she has caused him but quietly says "I can't tell you how".
Before she can say anything further, Caldicott interrupts her and says "Please, I only wish I could help you, that's all"

"Same here" adds Charters.

She smiles at the two noble English men and says "Thank you" and turns to face Caldicott to say "Goodbye Mr Caldicott".

"Goodbye Miss Whatsit" he fondly replies with a smile.

Charters and Caldicott follow Hogan the servant as he leads them to their room for the night.

A funny sort of holiday

In the bedroom, Charters and Caldicott are provided with further comfort that one would expect if staying unexpectedly with friends, in the form of pyjamas and dressing gowns. Charters removes his dressing gown, throws it over a chair and climbs into the double bed that Caldicott is already ensconced in.

Settling beside Caldicott, Charters says "A funny sort of position to be in"

"Yes" agrees his friend, "a funny sort of holiday"

"A funny sort of business altogether, I never thought that it would finish like this"

"Neither did I" agrees Caldicott.

Sitting side by side, propped up in the bed, the two English men consider their position. Charters asks "I wonder if Edith will ever hear about this?"

"I don't suppose anybody will hear anything about it ever again" says Caldicott rather disconsolately.

They continue to sit there pondering the events and their eventual fate, but they are soon distracted from their deliberations when they hear a slight noise at the door. They both look over, to see that a piece of paper has been pushed under the door. Caldicott quickly scrambles out of bed to retrieve it and returns to the bed with the note.

Charters whispers "What does it say?".

"There is just a chance" explains Caldicott

The smiling Charters queries his friend and asks "Caldicott?".

Caldicott continues reading the note, "We have a friend here who will try to substitute blank bullets".

"Good heavens!" exclaims Charters excitedly, once more interrupting his friend.

Caldicott continues to read the note "But he may not succeed".

Disturbed by this last comment, Charters stops smiling and says "Oh dear"

"When the shots are fired" continues Caldicott, "fall at once. Wait two minutes, then go to the gate in the west wall. It will be unlocked. Signed D"

"D?" queries Charters.

"Miss Deering" explains Caldicott, suddenly realising who the note is from and that there is a good chance that their lives might be saved. He turns to his friend, sitting next to him in the bed, and says "I say Charters, this is wonderful"

Not entirely convinced of how wonderful the plan is, Charters asks "Yes, but suppose this fellow doesn't put the blanks in?"

"Well" explains Caldicott matter of factly "we still fall"

Despite the threat of being shot in the morning, but possibly due to the note offering a glimmer of hope from the horrific tragedy that awaits them, the two friends soon get to sleep. Unfortunately, morning swiftly comes. Dressed, the two Englishmen find themselves in the courtyard waiting for the firing squad. However, not wanting to spoil their suits entirely with bullet holes and blood, they decide not to wear their jackets nor their collars and ties. Slowly, but surely, they are marched across the courtyard accompanied by soldiers forming the firing squad. The German officer in charge of the proceedings instructs them "You may stand with your back to the wall". Charters and Caldicott both look around to check their position relative to the wall. Happy with what they see, they turn to face the officer.

He says to them "Now gentlemen, you may have the choice"

"Choice?" asks Charters, hopefully.

"What of being shot or not?" asks Caldicott for clarification.

"Of bandage or no bandage" clarifies the officer sternly, not appreciating the humour; humour that he, as a German officer, considers inappropriate, at any time, never mind in these particular circumstances..

"No bandage" says Charters firmly. Caldicott looks at his friend, agrees with him and adds "No bandage" but not as firmly and tuts.

"Very good" says the officer, standing to attention before marching across to where the firing squad are moving into position facing the two prisoners. The officer raises his sword and the drums start beating a roll.

"Well goodbye old man; just in case" says Caldicott to his friend and raises his eyebrows as if looking to the heavens for help.

Charters quickly looks at his friend and replies "Goodbye Caldicott" before once more turning to face his executioners across the courtyard. The drums momentarily continue beating a roll. At the very instant that the beat stops, there is a loud volley of gunfire as the firing squad shoot Charters and Caldicott. The two Englishmen fall deathly to the hard surface of the courtyard.

Sometime later, the firing squad, having completed the death sentence of the two prisoners, has left. The courtyard is deathly quiet and the only evidence of the firing squad that remains is the smell of gunpowder lingering in the air and the seemingly lifeless bodies of the two English prisoners lying face down in the sand. Nothing moves and nothing is heard.

"This friend must have been able to shove in those blanks" whispers the very still Charters to an equally still Caldicott.
"Apparently" whispers back his friend, "see anybody about?"
"No" replies Charters with his face still buried in the sand.
"Ready to get up?" asks Caldicott.
"Yes" replies Charters, "we'd better make for that gate in the west wall; come on"
Charters and Caldicott slowly raise their heads from the floor to scan the courtyard before climbing to their feet. Soon standing, they rush across the courtyard towards the west gate. There they see Miss Deering waiting in a car for them with a driver; they quickly climb in beside and the car speeds off. Charters and Caldicott keep a watchful eye on the road behind them to see whether they are being followed or not. There isn't time for any explanation as to how or who swapped the bullets for blanks or even how Miss Deering escaped from her captors.
Miss Deering shouts to the driver "We must hurry, there's no time to lose. We must get that message to the airport before midnight"
Charters turns to speak to the driver "Go on, step on it old man"

Charters and Caldicott face the German firing squad

Escaped from the castle, and having passed the secret plans to the British Consul, the German plans to destroy Britain's oil interests in the Middle East have been thwarted. Their duty to King and Country done, Charters and Caldicott make their way back to England, travelling first class in an Express train, accompanied by Miss Deering. Sitting there in their first class compartment, Charters reads the papers in order to catch up on the latest cricket scores whilst Caldicott and Miss Deering are deep in conversation. "Well, soon be there now Miss Deering" says Caldicott, "London at last eh?"

Miss Deering smiles and is about to say something until Charters interrupts her, "Too late for the West Indies Test match though"

"Well, we'll still be able to see them play against Sussex old man" replies Caldicott; Charters nods in agreement.

"I expect the whole Foreign Office will be waiting to welcome you?" asks Caldicott, "after all that you've done for them"

Miss Deering smiles politely and modestly says "Oh, oh, we are not given recognition and we don't expect any"

"Well, I think it's a shame" says Caldicott, "after all that you've been through"

"I don't know what I would have done without both of you" says Miss Deering.

Caldicott smiles at this compliment and replies "I'd hardly go as far as to say that"

Charters agrees and adds "Oh, just a little initiative, common sense, you know"

"Well erm, I suppose your fiancé will be waiting for you Mr Caldicott?" asks Miss Deering.

"Oh, that's not likely" he replies.

"Highly unlikely" adds Charters with a wry smile, not entirely disappointed that his friend is no longer engaged to be married to his sister Edith..

"Yes" says Caldicott, "even if there's no official welcome, I suppose there'll be somebody waiting for you"

"Oh no" laughs Miss Deering, "that's even more unlikely"

"Is it really?" asks Caldicott, smiling with renewed interest at this latest piece of information. He lovingly looks into her eyes. She returns the smile, Caldicott adds "If you are going to be all alone, I mean, I'm not engaged or anything, and I thought perhaps we could, err"

Miss Deering, still smiling at Caldicott, replies "Perhaps, we could, err"

"Shall we?" asks Caldicott who is now grinning widely.

Miss Deering murmurs smiles and nods at Caldicott. They are both clearly madly in love with each other. Caldicott breaks from gazing at Miss Deering to lean over to Charters who, though still reading his newspaper, looks up and winks his approval with an added grin.

Caldicott positions himself closer to Miss Deering by raising the arm rest that separates them and puts his arm around her. They embrace and he kisses her; she responds to his love and returns the kiss with great affection.

Charters gives his blessing to Caldicott's romance with Miss Deering.

Millions Like Us

On the safe side

Everywhere is in darkness but through the gloom, faint shadows give away clues as to where Charters and Caldicott are. Even without any light, there is sufficient clarity in the various noises emanating from every corner of the darkness to easily give the location. Charters and Caldicott are at the central railway station trying to find the correct platform from where their train will depart to take them to their next commission.

With a little help from the hand torch that Caldicott has cleverly remembered, they find the platform where their train is waiting. Slowly but surely, and with the additional help of the platform guard, they find a first class compartment on the awaiting train that is empty. This is exactly what they were looking for, an empty first class compartment which permits smoking and empty. This is how Charters and Caldicott prefer to travel, first class, no other passengers – all adding up to a peaceful journey where they can enjoy a quiet puff on their pipes whilst they contemplate and discuss things of importance to them.

The announcement confirms that they have found the correct train – Basingstoke, Winchester, Southampton, Bournemouth, Hamworthy, Wareham and Dorchester. The announcement goes on to say that the special evacuation train for the Dorset and Hampshire areas are standing at platforms 3, 5 and 7 is also heard. But Charters and Caldicott pay no attention to this announcement as they have found their train; after all the evacuees were sent down during the day and they are travelling at night.

Caldicott enters the compartment first, flashing the torch around in order to find the best spot, closely followed by his old friend Charters. They are both dressed in army uniform, Charters that of a captain and Caldicott in a similar uniform with one less pip befitting of a lieutenant.

Its blackout and Charters and Caldicott look for an empty compartment

As Caldicott puts his case on the luggage rack above him, charters struggles with his luggage in to the compartment and closes the door behind him. The closure of the door whilst dulling the noises outside the carriage, it doesn't fully block out all the noise, particularly when there is a group of soldiers nearby on the platform singing whilst waiting to board their train. Charters finds a home for his luggage; he has brought more than Caldicott and it doesn't go unnoticed. "You seem to be taking a lot of stuff with you old man. How long do you think this war is going to last?" asks Caldicott.

"Nothing like being on the safe side Caldicott" replies his friend slightly disparagingly. He is already tired from carrying his luggage without the aid of a porter through the darkened but very busy railway station. Having put his case on the shelf next to his friend's, he throws a bag on to the seat opposite him, sits down next to Caldicott and looks for his pipe in his jacket pockets.

"Personally, I think it will be all over by Christmas" says Caldicott hopefully.

Taking his pipe out of his mouth in order to reply, Charters looks at Caldicott and chuckles "ha, ha., that's what people said during the last war"

"Well last time people said it would be over by Christmas and it wasn't" replies Caldicott, "but this time it might be" still hopeful in what the future might hold.

Charters glances at Caldicott, contemplating about what he just said. As he fills his pipe, he says "Mmm, I doubt if that is very sound logic old man" and continues to light his pipe, puffing away to get the tobacco burring.

The conversation is loudly interrupted by by a shrill noise emanating from just outside the compartment on the platform; it is a woman shouting at a group of children following in her wake. "Now come along, stop chatting and keep together" she shouts.

Caldicott looks through the windows on both sides of the compartment to see what the commotion is and where the noise is coming from. "I thought that they were running special trains all day, evacuating children" Caldicott says.

"yes they were" replies his friend, "perhaps they were some of them left over" indicating with his hand, the group of children he can see outside on the platform. "Anyway, we needn't worry; this is a first class compartment"

The shrill sound of the woman's voice gets louder as she gets nearer to Charters and Caldicott's compartment. They hear her shouting more instructions to the children; firstly by shouting their names to better get their attention before shouting "Come along, come and get in here" and opens the compartment door where Charters and Caldicott are sitting looking very worried. She starts to help the children into the

171

compartment, the first one being a small boy who she lifts up and passes to Charters. Charters is not happy about this intrusion into their compartment and looks away in order to avoid eye contact with the woman, hoping that the situation will not develop any further.

"Do you mind taking him?" the woman says to Charters. The young boy is swiftly followed by a growing group of loud noisy children. "Ten more" the woman says to the children waiting on the platform. Charters, having reluctantly taken the boy off the woman, quickly passes him on to an equally worried looking Caldicott.

An evacuee spoils the peace and quiet in the compartment.

The group of very noisy children bustle into the compartment, pushing past each other and in the process bumping and teetering into Charters and Caldicott. The two officers are squashed in to their compartment with more than a dozen very noisy children who are in the process of being evacuated. What was, minutes before, a very quiet and private first class compartment occupied solely by Charters and Caldicott has become the equivalent of a third class carriage converted into an unruly and disorganised kindergarten.

The train, having been populated with even more evacuees and passengers, is now full to the brim in every available space. Not only is Charters and Caldicott's compartment full, but so is every available space, including the corridors and luggage carriages; full with evacuees, soldiers travelling to and from their postings and other assorted fellow travellers. The train finally pulls out of the railway station on its journey through the countryside and onwards to Eastbourne and the coast.

On the beach

Soon after signing up for service in the army, Charters and Caldicott are given their first posting; they are responsible for fortifying a stretch of the coast line along the south coast, or rather in the vicinity of Eastbourne to be precise. Their work is build up Britain's coastal defences to thwart any possible invasion force that Hitler might send across the English Channel. Captain Charters and Lieutenant Caldicott and their unit are on the beach burying land mines just below the surface of the sand. Caldicott watches the men at work whilst Charters makes notes on the exact position of where each mines is laid. However, doing their duty doesn't prevent them from having a conversation.

"And when I got home" says Caldicott turning to look at Charters, "there was my wife entertaining two Czech officers to tea"

"Really" says Charters only half listening to his friend as he concentrates on writing down the position of the latest mine to be laid in the sand. He finishes writing and adds "Talking of war time sacrifices Caldicott, you remember old Patterinson?" and taps his pencil on Caldicott's shoulder to regain his friend's attention.

"The chap with all those rubber plantations in Malaya?" asks Caldicott.

"Yes, that's the fellow" confirms Charters, "You remember his valet, Hawkins?"

"Yes" replies his friend.

"He's evacuated to Weston-Super-Mare" says Charters

"Really" exclaims Caldicott, glad that he has never been asked to go to Weston-Super-Mare.

"Patterinson is absolutely livid" adds Charters, "he hasn't dressed himself in over thirty years"

"What's he going to do about it?" asks Caldicott.

173

"Follow him to Weston-Super-Mare" confirms Charters still surprised at his old friend's bravery in going there.

Charters and Caldicott are supervising the laying of mines on the beach.

"Oh, by the way" says Caldicott glancing around and thinking that they may have momentarily stopped concentrating on the task in hand, "how many mines have we laid this morning?"
Charters looks around as he gives the matter some thought before saying "mm eighty six, err no eighty seven"
"Sure?" asks Caldicott.
"Positive" comes the reply
Not sure whether or not he trusts his friend's confidence at counting mines nor recording their positions accurately, Caldicott has another look around him and says "We must remember not to bathe here after the war". They both look across the beach; Charters wondering if there is something in what his friend has just said,

On the train

Charters and Caldicott are once more on the train to Eastbourne, and once again the train is full; it is full to the point that every available space is taken. Passengers are standing and sitting wherever they can find a square foot of floor or even a wall to lean against. Charters and Caldicott are not used to this type of travel; they can't even get into any of the first or second class carriages and are having to travel third class; even worse is that the only space they can find is a tightly packed corridor. Still everybody else is in the same boat; or as Caldicott would probably point out if Charters had said it – everybody is on the same train!

The two officers, standing in the corridor, are trying to eat some sandwiches, when Charters has a thought, "Remember old Patterinson?" he asks.
"What the fellow that used to have all those rubber plantations in Malaya?" Caldicott replies.
"Mmm, that's right" says Charters, "Don't you remember, I told you I saw him once standing in a third class corridor eating salmon sandwiches"
"mm" agrees Caldicott.
"Well, we're doing it now old boy" says Charters, indicating the sandwiches in his hand.
"No, these are sardine paste" says Caldicott taking the conversation quite literally and correcting his friend.

"Are they" asks Charters now unsure of what he is actually eating or rather the taste is not what he expects. He looks at his sandwich before putting his nose close to see if he distinguish the flavour by smell. "Oh!" he adds, "I see what you mean"

There is nothing more that can be said, Charters anecdote about his friend eating salmon sandwiches on the train has now lost its meaning; Charters and Caldicott continue their train journey to back to Eastbourne in silence, stile ting their sardine paste sandwiches but not particularly enjoying them.

175

Standing room only on the train

Film information

The Lady Vanishes (1938)

Night Train To Munich (1940)

Crook's Tour (1941)

Millions Like Us (1943)

The Lady Vanishes (1938)

Directed by Alfred Hitchcock

This 1938 movie follows the exploits of a beautiful young English lady, Iris Henderson as she returns from her holiday in Europe to travel back to Britain to marry her fiancée. The train that she is planning to catch is delayed due to a snow avalanche and forced to stop overnight. Her friends, Julie and Blanche come with her to wave her off the next day; all three stay the night at the "Gasthof Petrus" inn in the fictitious Eastern European country of Bandrika. Bandrika is evidently involved in the political circumstances leading up to the start of the Second World War with espionage and secrecy being high on the agenda. Other travellers are also forced to stay the night at the inn including Charters and Caldicott, They too are returning to England, but their reason is to get back in time to watch the last days of a cricket test match between England and Australia.

The inn is full to capacity with all the unexpected guests and Charters and Caldicott end up being allocated Anna the maid's room as they are the last to register their stay. During the night's stay at the inn, Iris who regularly stays there with her two friends, complains about the loud music coming from the room above her, where Gilbert, a young music anthropologist, is playing a folk tune to accompany two local folk dancers. The manager likes to keep his regular guests happy, particularly the wealthy ones such as Iris and her friends; he acts on her complaint, by asking Gilbert to leave his room. Correctly guessing who made the complaint, he attempts to move into Iris's room, much to her annoyance. He is eventually reinstated back to his own room. Meanwhile, Miss Froy, a former governess and music teacher, sits at her open window in order to listen to a secret message hidden in a tune performed by a folk violinist under her window.

The next morning, as she is about to board the train, Iris is hit on the head by a planter pushed from the hotel roof; the planter was aimed at Miss Froy. Miss Froy helps Iris onto the train and share a compartment where they befriend each other; other travelers in the first class compartment include a Baroness, Signor Doppo and his wife amongst others. During the journey, Iris joins Miss Froy for tea in the dining car where Charters and Caldicott are also having tea whilst deep in conversation about a cricket match.

On returning to their compartment, Iris falls asleep, but on awakening, Miss Froy has disappeared. The other travellers in her compartment deny having seen Miss Froy, and despite her frantic requests from Miss Henderson refuse to believe or help her. Seemingly alone, Iris searches for the missing lady, trying the next compartment where a lawyer Mr. Todhunter and his mistress, travelling under the pseudonym of his wife are seated. Not wanting to bring any attention to their adulterous affair, they deny any knowledge of Miss Froy. Charters and Caldicott also deny having seen Miss Froy, because they are afraid that any further delay will result in them missing the cricket match.

Iris continues looking for Miss Froy, eventually meeting up with the annoying Gilbert, who is travelling in the second class carriages. Although they took a dislike to each other after the previous night's falling out, he eventually agrees to help her. One of the other travellers on the train is an eminent brain surgeon, Dr. Hartz. After listening to her story, he concludes that Iris is suffering from concussion-related hallucinations. Gilbert, still skeptical about the story of the missing lady, sees some sense in this explanation, but Iris is not convinced.

The conspirators behind Miss Froy's disappearance try to pass off another elderly lady, Madame Kummer, as the missing Miss Froy. Neither Iris, nor Gilbert, are convinced. Finding evidence of Miss Froy's existence, Gilbert finally believes Iris, and continues searching with her. They look along the full length of the train, including the luggage compartment, where they crates belonging to a magician, Signor Doppo. Whilst searching them, they find themselves attacked by the knife-wielding magician.

They soon come to the conclusion that Miss Froy has been abducted by Dr. Hartz who has disguised her as his unconscious patient by bandaging her face completely. The patient is being cared for by a nun working for Dr. Hartz; he tells her to kill Iris and Gilbert. Fortunately, the nun is unhappy with how the conspiracy is developing so does not follow the Doctor's instructions, but allows Gilbert and Iris to escape.

Upon freeing Miss Froy, they replace the bandaged patient with one of the other conspirators.

Dr. Hartz discovers the switch when he arranges for the bandaged patient to be moved into a waiting ambulance. On realising what has happened, he and his military counterparts split the train carriages into two, and divert the section containing Miss Froy and the other English travelers who are all having afternoon tea. The dining car, containing the English travelers, is diverted onto a branch line, where armed troops await. Iris and Gilbert warn their fellow passengers what is happening, but not everybody believes them. The Officer in charge of the military force boards the train to convince the passengers to surrender, but Gilbert overpowers him. Mr. Todhunter is not convinced about Iris's story and attempts to surrender to avoid a diplomatic incident. Alighting from the train, waving a white handkerchief, he is shot dead.

During the ensuing gunfight, Miss Froy escapes in to the woods but not before revealing to Iris and Gilbert, that she is a British agent with a secret message to deliver to the Foreign Office. The message is encoded in the tune that Miss Froy heard the folk singer singing at the Inn; she entrusts the tune to Iris and Gilbert. The remaining passengers, including Charters and Caldicott devise a plan to commandeer the locomotive, reset the track points and eventually escape across the border to safety.

Back in London, Charters and Caldicott are disappointed to discover that despite all their efforts to get back to England on time, the Test Match was cancelled. Iris avoids her waiting fiancée by going to the Foreign Office with Gilbert. Unfortunately, Gilbert cannot remember the tune when they get to the Foreign Office; that is until he and Iris hear the tune being played on a piano in an adjoining room. It is Miss Froy playing the tune; she has also safely escaped back to England.

Alfred Hitchcock is seen towards the end of the film as the travelers alight at Victoria Station; he is wearing a black coat and smoking a cigarette.

Writing Credits

Sidney Gilliat and Frank Launder

Based upon the 1936 story: "The Wheel Spins" by Ethel Lina White

Cast

Caldicott	Naunton Wayne
Charters	Basil Radford
Iris Henderson	Margaret Lockwood
Gilbert	Michael Redgrave
Dr. Hartz	Paul Lukas
Miss Froy	Dame May Whitty
Mr. Todhunter	Cecil Parker
'Mrs' Todhunter	Linden Travers
Baroness	Mary Clare
Hotel Manager	Emile Boreo
Blanche	Googie Withers
Julie	Sally Stewart
Signor Doppo (magician)	Philip Leaver
Signora Doppo	Selma Vaz Dias
The Nun	Catherine Lacey
Madame Kummer	Josephine Wilson
The Officer	Charles Oliver
Anna	Kathleen Tremaine
Man in London Railway Station	Alfred Hitchcock
Violinist	Roy Russell

Filming Locations

Train scenes	Hampshire, England, UK
Train scenes	Longmoor Military Camp and Railway, Hampshire, England, UK

184

Train scenes	Woolmer Forest, Hampshire, England, UK
Studios	Gaumont-British Studios, Shepherd's Bush London, England UK
Studios	Gaumont-British Studios, Islington, London, England, UK
Gasthof Petrus Inn	Scale Model

Night Train to Munich (1940)

Directed by Carol Reed

The film opens at The Berhof in Germany, Hitler's mountain retreat. The Fuhrer is yelling at his Generals and screaming about Austria and the Sudetenland. Acting on his orders, the might of the German army invade neighbouring countries and grab bits and pieces of Europe thereby expanding the German Reich. It is the time of the "Phoney War", the period at the start of World War II that was marked by a lack of major military operations by the Western Allies against the German Reich.

Inventor Axel Bomasch has to flee from Czechoslovakia, moments before the German army invade. As an inventor of new armour plating steel, he has been warned that the Nazis are looking for him to take him captive so that he will work for them in helping their war effort. Whilst he escapes, his daughter Anna does not and is captured and put to work as a nurse in a concentration camp. The Germans stage-manage a meeting of Anna and inmate Karl Marsen just as he is being beaten by the guards. The German plan succeeds, and Anna forms a friendship with him, revealing that she is the daughter of an inventor wanted by the Germans. Marsen devises an escape plan for the two of them after Anna tells Marsen that she wants to escape to safety across the border into Switzerland.

They successfully flee their prison and cross Europe to safety in England. As Anna tries to find her father, she receives a message that will help her. She is told to seek out Gus Bennett, a singer and salesman of popular songs at a seaside resort. Unbeknown to her, Bennett is also a secret agent, but working for the British Intelligence. He is suspicious of how Anna was able to escape from Germany so easily; rightfully so, when he realizes that Marsen is a German agent. Marsen's plans were to get Anna out of Germany in order to find and capture her father; he then succeeds in spiriting him and his daughter back to the fatherland.

187

Bennett goes undercover as a high ranking German military engineer and travels to Germany in order to rescue Anna and her father and return them to England.

Unable to convince them of the merits of working for Germany, the military officers hand the two over to the Gestapo where they are to be taken to Munich for further interrogation. Before they are handed over, Bennett, in disguise as a German officer manages to infiltrate the local military command and convince them that he has been ordered to form part of the escorting party.

Meanwhile, Charters and Caldicott are travelling through Europe as their holiday comes to a close. It is the time of the "Phoney War" and whilst the two are aware of military activities in Germany, they do not feel threatened by them, as Britain and Germany are not yet at war with each other. They are on their way back to England keen to catch the last days of the cricket test match that England are playing in. They board the same train as the Bomaschs' and their military escort, but not before purchasing a copy of Mein Kampf from the station news stall. During the journey, Caldicott thinks that he recognizes Bennett, not as Bennett nor as a German Officer, but as Dickie Randall, an old school friend.

The train makes an unscheduled stop where all passengers have to leave the train, due to it being commandeered by the military for troop deployment. Now that he has the opportunity, Caldicott goes to greet his old school chum Dickie Randall. On being asked, Bennett, or Dickie Randall, denies knowing Caldicott or the person he believes him to be, leaving Caldicott mortified and Charters embarrassed. Charters and Caldicott, having found somewhere to sit whilst they wait for a replacement train, are moved from waiting room to platform bench again and again, by a series of guards and a bossy Station Guard. In the process they find out that war has been declared and Britain is now at war with Germany. Charters is less concerned about war itself than he is about recovering a set of golf clubs loaned to an old friend before war makes it impossible to recover them. Whilst trying to make a telephone call to his European friend, he interrupts the Gestapo officer speaking with his headquarters and overhears a conversation revealing that the Germans know that Bennett is not who he says he is and that they plan to arrest him when the train arrives at Munich.

Initially thinking bad of him, for seemingly being part of the German war effort, they now know that Dickie Randall is in fact also distrusted by the Germans and that he needs to be warned about the dangers facing him. Back on the train, they devise a plan to get a message to him and explain what Charters overheard.

Randall meets clandestinely with Charters and Caldicott; between them they hatch a cunning plan to not only save Dickie Randall but also to achieve his original plan of rescuing the Bomaschs' from the clutches of the Third Reich. Overpowering the German officers and guards, Charters and Caldicott accompany Dickie Randall in releasing the inventor and his daughter from their captors. The next part of the plan involves Charters and Caldicott swapping their clothes for those of German soldiers thereby supporting Dickie Randall in his disguise as a senior officer. The three Englishmen, dressed as German soldiers, successfully escort the Bomaschs' from the train evading the awaiting armed escort and then commandeer a waiting military car that had been arranged to take the Bomaschs' to Gestapo Headquarters.

A chase to the boundary with Switzerland subsequently ensues as the Germans realize that they have been duped. Randall directs the car at high speed to an unguarded border point he knows of, where a teleferic cable car lift stretches between Germany and Switzerland. Here the final battle occurs as the Germans catch the fleeing group mid flight.

Writing Credits

Sidney Gilliat and Frank Launder

Based on the original story "Report on a Fugitive", by Gordon Wellesley

Cast

| Charters | Basil Radford |
| Caldecott | Naunton Wayne |

Anna Bomasch	Margaret Lockwood
Gus Bennett	Rex Harrison
Karl Marsen	Paul Henreid
Axel Bomasch	James Harcourt
Dr. Fredericks	Felix Aylmer
Dryton	Wyndham Goldie
Roberts	Roland Culver
Schwab	Eliot Makeham
Kampenfeldt	Raymond Huntley
Capt. Prada	Austin Trevor
Controller	Kenneth Kent
Admiral Hassinger	C.V. France
Gestapo Officer	Frederick Valk
Teleferic Attendant	Morland Graham
Minor Role	Edward Baxter
Minor Role	Jane Cobb
Deckchair Attendant	Arthur Denton
Official at Home Office, MI5	Ian Fleming
Station Master	Irene Handl
Inspector on Train	Bryan Herbert
Himself (archive footage)	Adolf Hitler
Official at Prague Steel Works	David Horne
Prisoner in Concentration Camp	Allan Jeayes
Concentration Camp Guard	Albert Lieven
SS Officer Checking Passes	Howard Marion-Crawford
Minor Role	G.H. Mulcaster
SS Officer - Concentration Camp	Charles Oliver
Minor Role	Winifred Oughton
Fisherman	Wally Patch

Minor Role	J.H. Roberts
Adolf Hitler	Billy Russell
Minor Role	Torin Thatcher
Official at Prague Steel Works	Wilfred Walter
Concentration Camp Physician	John Wengraf
Train Steward	Ben Williams
Minor Role	Pat Williams
Minor Role	Padre Woodman

Filming Locations

Studio	Gaumont-British Studios, Shepherd's Bush London, England UK
The Berhof	Scale model

Crook's Tour (1941)

Directed by John Baxter

On holiday again, Charters and Caldicott are in the Middle East touring with Spindles Tours. Part way through the journey, the charabanc that they are travelling, in runs out of fuel. Whilst the tour guide apologises profusely, there is nothing that can be done; they and the other travelers are stranded in the middle of the desert in Saudi Arabia. Fortunately, a passing Sheik and his entourage come across the stranded group; he turns out to be an alma mater of Charters; they both studied at the same school. Charters and Caldicott are fortunate in finding a friend to rescue them from being marooned in the desert. Over dinner that evening, they are offered the use of two camels to help them continue their journey to Baghdad. Before they can mount the camels, the Sheik's aides manage to repair the charabanc. Charters and Caldicott resume their journey as planned, without having to resort to a form of travel that they are not entirely familiar with.

At Baghdad Railway Station, they have some time to spare before their connecting train leaves, so the two look for somewhere suitable to dine. Finding a poster advertising a restaurant with entertainment, Charters and Caldicott set off to find it. At the restaurant, Caldicott is mesmerized by a singer dancer called La Palermo. She not only sings but dances seductively around the dance floor removing her numerous veils one by one, throwing them over the guests. Caldicott is the recipient of the final veil to be removed. Charters is enraged with Caldicott's inappropriate behavior as he is engaged to be married to Edith, Charters' sister.

Whilst dining, they are mistaken for German agents, and Caldicott is sold in error, a gramophone record. Unbeknown to the two Englishmen, the record contains information vital to Britain's enemies.

The two English men catch their train to Istanbul on route to Budapest, where Charters' sister Edith is due to meet them. Having found out that Charters and Caldicott are not spies, and have been given the record by mistake, the two are pursued to Istanbul by Nazi agents, desperate to recover the gramophone record. Charters and

Caldicott are reluctantly persuaded to go to the Hamilton hotel by a tour guide they meet outside the railway station. Despite having the appearance of an ordinary hotel in the heart of Istanbul, The Hamilton is actually owned and operated by the Nazis. There, the two travellers see La Palermo again, singing and dancing in the hotel's restaurant bar.

The attractive singer warns them they are in danger, but unsure of the meaning of what she says, they ignore her advice; that is, until they foil a trap intended to kill Caldicott. The trap involves a deep drop through an open hole just inside the bathroom doorway. Charters sees a man, presuming him to be Caldicott fall through the hole and into the Bosporus deep below. Charters is distraught about his friend, considering himself responsible as it was he who tapped the man on the shoulder before he fell. Fortunately, it transpires that it wasn't Caldicott as he comes sauntering down the corridor to see what all the fuss is about.

Unimpressed by service in Istanbul, particularly the bathroom arrangements, Charters and Caldicott head to Budapest, still followed by the German spy Rossenger, La Palermo and other Nazi spies.

On arriving in Budapest, Charters and Caldicott find a hotel but insist on checking that the bathrooms have baths. Exhausted with fatigue after travelling for what seems like ages, as well as the shock of the man been killed by falling through the bathroom floor, the two Englishmen go straight to bed. During the night, they are both awoken unexpectedly, but for different reasons. Charters receives a phone call from his irate sister, Edith, demanding him to get out of bed and explain why she hasn't been informed of where to meet them as originally planned. In the room next door, Caldicott is awoken by an intruder trying to steal the gramophone record. As he tries to ascertain why the woman is in his bedroom stealing his belongings, he realizes that the intruder is none other than La Palermo. Before she has the chance to explain, Charters and his sister Edith walk into the bedroom. They are both disgusted at what they see; Edith because her fiancé has an attractive woman in his bedroom and Charters because of what he sees as a betrayal of his sister and also his friendship - the engagement is off.

Wanting to get to the bottom of the incidents that have befallen him, Charters agrees to help Caldicott. Listening to the record that the intruder tried to steal, they realize that it contains a secret message concerning the Nazis' plans to destroy an oil pipeline that the British have an interest in. Whilst they consider what to do with their findings, they are given a message to come to a secret meeting next day. It is La Palermo who meets them; despite their misgivings about her being a spy, she convinces them that she is working for British Intelligence and that she wants them to give the record to one of her colleagues, Captain Spanswick.

Unbeknown to La Palermo, the real Captain Spanswick is dead; she doesn't find out the truth until it is too late and the record has been handed over. Unfortunately Charters and Caldicott have heard the record and know of the message; the Germans need to silence them and therefore set a trap to capture them. The bait is La Palermo and the trap is at a remote castle. Charters and Caldicott fall for the trap and are captured; the Nazis intend to shoot them and transfer La Palermo to Nazi headquarters for further interrogation. However the British Intelligence service also has a plan; Charters, Caldicott and La Palermo are rescued.

It also transpires that Charters and Caldicott gave the wrong record to the German spy disguised as Captain Spanswick; the British agents obtain the correct copy and Germany's plans to destroy the oil pipeline are thwarted.

Writing Credits

Screenplay by John Watt and Max Kester

Script by Barbara K. Emary,

Based on original Radio Story by Frank Launder and Sidney Gilliat

Cast

Charters	Basil Radford
Caldicott	Naunton Wayne
La Palermo	Greta Gynt

Ali	Abraham Sofaer
Sheik	Charles Oliver
Rossenger	Gordon McLeod
Klacken	Bernard Rebel
K.7.	Cyril Gardiner
Waiter	Morris Harvey
Edith Charters	Noel Hood
Hotel Manager	Leo de Pokorny
American	Cyril Chamberlain
Tourist on Desert Bus	Finlay Currie
Bit Role	Peter Gawthorne
Nightclub Manager	Andreas Malandrinos
Hotel Receptionist	Patricia Medina
Desert Bus Tour Guide	Jack Melford
Manservant at Castle	Charles Rolfe
Bit Role	Bill Shine

Filming Locations

Rock Studios, Borehamwood, Hertfordshire, England, UK

Millions Like Us (1943)

Directed by Sidney Gilliat and Frank Launder

Millions Like US is a moving dramatisation of life on the British home front at the start of the Second World War. The film opens with the city dwelling Crowson family setting off on their annual holiday to the British seaside resort of Eastbourne, where they stay at the same bed and breakfast 'hotel' as they have always done for many years before. It is 1939 and shortly after the holiday, Britain, deciding that enough is enough, declares war on Germany.

The Crowson family are no different from the millions of other families whose life's are to be changed. They are a lower middle class family led by Jim Crowson, who is married to his second wife Elsie, who lives with his two daughters from his first marriage, Phyllis and Celia. His son, who is never shown, is away in one of the services. Whilst men are called up for active duty, it is largely the women of Britain that are left to keep the home front going by fulfilling the roles left by their men folk. Jim's wife Elsie, has to return to her job as a switchboard operator due to staff shortages and the spotlight soon turns on the daughters as the need for them to contribute to the war effort soon arrives.

Phyllis announces that she is going to join the WAAFS and Celia receives a letter asking her to turn up for an interview at the Labour Exchange. Celia dreams of driving senior officers around or nursing the wounded and receiving a marriage proposal from one of her handsome patients. In reality, the call-up results in her being posted to work in an armament factory making vital parts for war planes. Initially disappointed with her allotted role, she nevertheless reports for duty, travelling by train to the remote aircraft engineering factory. She soon makes friends with a friendly but disparate group of fellow workers from a variety of social classes. The group comprises Jennifer, a middle-class city girl, cynical and wise in the ways of the world; Brenda, a northern tomboy without any airs or graces or indeed much in clothes or personal possessions and Gwen an intelligent Welsh girl who has left university to help with the war effort..

Life at the factory and hostel, where the girls live, soon develops to a

197

regular harmonious momentum of factory work followed by tea dances and social events including the weekly dance where airmen from the nearby airfield join the ladies for tea, dancing and friendship. Celia meets, and soon falls in love with Fred Blake a young Scottish airman and the snooty Jennifer develops a love hate relationship with the factory supervisor, the dour and straight talking Charlie Forbes. After admonishing her for not going to the shelter during an air raid, Charlie picks her up and carries her over his shoulder for her own safety to the shelter. Much to her initial reticence, she realises her attraction to him.

Whilst Celia and Fred agree to marry, Jennifer and Charlie sensibly realise that their differences in background and outlook on life may be too much of a barrier to prevent them from ever marrying each other, and they settle for a friendly and endeared relationship, unsure, but not worried, of what the future holds for them.

Having seen his daughter married to Fred without much pomp or ceremony, Jim Crowson continues living his life without any women in the house; old-fashioned that he is, Jim struggles to keep his house in order. Treading unfamiliar territory, he fails to eat or cook properly and the whole house soon becomes untidy with every conceivable piece of crockery, cutlery or cooking utensil remaining dirty and unclean for days on end. Rather than the wholesome home cooked meals he was accustomed to before the war, his staple diet now consists mainly of pies, chips and other greasy food from whichever cafe he can find.

Meanwhile, Charters and Caldicott have also been called up to serve their country and are commissioned officers in the army, Charters holding the rank of Captain and Caldicott a Lieutenant. Travelling away from the city to take up their posting in Eastbourne, and as befitting, English gentlemen and officers, they travel by first class. Unfortunately their journey is disrupted by a large group of children who are being evacuated to safer lives in the countryside and seaside away from the likely city targets. Their first class carriage is soon full of noisy children; not how they are accustomed to travelling. Their commission at Eastbourne is to help erect a system of defences along the coast line in order to thwart any threat of invasion. Part of this remit is to lay landmines along the beaches on what was once a popular seaside town thronging with thousands of visitors each summer.

Unbeknown to them and the other characters, war won't be over before Christmas as they hope, and it will be some time before crowds of holidaymakers return to enjoy the sea and beach.

The whole film is a reflection on how charming life was, for the people of Britain before Hitler unleashed the horror of war across Europe. Life changed for many millions of people, from their annual holidays at the seaside and peaceful first class travel through to men leaving their families behind whilst they were shipped overseas to fight the enemy and women having to work in factories and coping with air raids. Even children's lives were changed forever, with the loss of parents either permanently or temporarily due to being evacuated to distant strange parts of the country. But right to the end, this rousing wartime propaganda film shows that the British remained strong, resilient and cheerful, and determined more than ever to overcome whatever hardships they had to face, to remain united in their lone stand against the might of the German army marching across Europe to the shores of Britain.

Writing Credits

Frank Launder and Sidney Gilliat

Cast

Charters	Basil Radford
Caldicott	Naunton Wayne
Celia Crowson	Patricia roc
Fred Blake	Gordon Jackson
Jennifer Knowles	Anne Crawford
Jim Crowson	Moor Marriott
Charlie Forbes	Eric Portman
Phyllis Crowson	Joy Shelton
Gwen Price	Megs Jenkins
Tom	John Boxer
Elsie	Valentine Dunn

Annie Earnshaw	Terry Randall
Mrs Blythe	Amy Veness
Doctor Gill	John Salew
Miss Wells	Beatrice Valex
Landlady	Irene Handl
Mrs Bourne	Amy Dalby
Brenda	Brenda Bruce

Filming Locations

Gainsborough Studios, London

Eastbourne and Oxfordshire, England, UK